No Longer a Prisoner

ALSO BY WENDY MASSEY

I'm Happy Being Me!

Happy Being Me Village,
Spiritually Charged -
Edition

Happy Being Me Village,
Freedom - Edition

The Whole Armor of God

No Longer a Prisoner

WENDY MASSEY

ISBN: 13: 978-0-578-46667-5
ISBN: 10: 0-578-46667-8

Library of Congress Control Number: 2019902452
Copyright © 2019 Wendy Massey.

Unless otherwise identified, scripture quotations are from
the King James Version, Bible.

Printed in the United States of America
Published by, Wendy Massey, Someone Cares About Me
www.someonecaresaboutme.com

To make a purchase or learn more about our Creative Writing & Publishing Services, visit **www.someonecaresaboutme.com**

Follow us:
Facebook @Someone Cares About Me LLC
YouTube @Wendy Inspire
YouTube @HAPPYBEINGME
Instagram @someonecaresaboutme

Creative Writing & Publishing Services

Every great journey begins with a single step. You have a story worth telling, and we're here to help you bring it to life. With our support, you can share your unique perspective with readers from all walks of life and inspire others to follow in your footsteps. Take that first step today and discover where your writing can take you! Our team will be here to cheer you on every step of the way.

Please reach out to schedule your complimentary writer's consultation!

Someone Cares About Me LLC
P. O. Box 2024
Aston, PA 19014

Dedications

This book is dedicated to Elohim, who has strengthened me through every twist and turn of life. I realize that the challenges I faced prepared me for this moment and for many greater things yet to come. I now know that I am equipped for anything that comes my way!

I would also like to express my heartfelt gratitude to my darling husband, Tarquin Massey, who loved me before I learned to love myself. Thank you for your understanding and gentle support.

To my son (My Gift From God) , Tarquan Massey who gave me the will to fight! I look forward to the day you realize how truly awesome you are!

My mother, Gerry Gaines who has always been there to dust me off each time I fell and reminded me to keep "movin' & shakin'."

My sister, Roslyne Kelsey who held my hand through the most difficult times of my life.

My first cousin, Antonio Jones, also known as Boss! Thank you for creating a safe space for me when I needed it the most!

To those who will continue The Massey Legacy, it's important to know our history. We were once kings and queens, and we have much to be proud of!

Lastly, to those who experienced dark moments and didn't think they would push past the pain yet are moving forward.

Cheers to the overcomers!

Acknowledgements

Thank you, D'Mont Reese Photography, for investing extra time to ensure we captured the perfect shot. Thank you for your patience, direction and professionalism.

I searched high and low for the best dress for my book cover. I purchased many dresses which I had to return because they did not support the vision. Thank you so much Beatrice Dufort for helping me find the right dress for the cover just a few days before my scheduled shoot. I truly appreciate you taking time out of your busy schedule to lend a hand.

Thank you to my cover illustrator for your patience as we worked together to bring this book to life.

Once again my pre-press and layout expert, Nabeel Tahir invested such detail and time in formatting this book for my valued readers. I can't thank you enough!

I'm grateful for my family, friends and The Happy Being Me Villagers who continue to support my hopes, dreams and aspirations...

I am excited that you're reading my book, and I hope that you will discover something new as you read through the chapters. My true desire is to inspire you and others!

This is my story.

The events described in this book reflect my personal beliefs and experiences. Others may perceive these events differently. I was initially hesitant to share my journey, fearing criticism from others. However, over time, I realized that if I don't share my story, all my hardships and dark moments would be in vain.

Although I wrote this book to free myself from the hurts of my past, I am also keen on encouraging others to do the same. We are all tightly interwoven and connected one way or the other. Thus, it is important that we recognize we inspire others to tackle and overcome challenges in their lives. We can all bask in the euphoria of a fulfilled life.

Some places, identifying characteristics and people's names have been changed or omitted to protect the privacy of those who have made mistakes. We all deserve a second chance.

Some events have been compressed, and some dialogue has been recreated. I wrote this book from a place of love, strength, and forgiveness. By no means do I wish for anyone to be negatively impacted by the sharing of my story.

Through this book, I aim to provide you with hope and reassurance that your past does not define your present, nor does it prevent you from achieving a better future.

Take a moment for deep introspection. Reflect on how far you have come! Consider the times you thought you wouldn't survive. Remember the moments when you struggled to make ends meet? Think back to when you believed there was no job out there for you. Do you recall when you thought you would never find love? You may have walked around with your head held low or cried yourself to sleep on many dark nights. But now, do you realize that you are still standing after all you've been through?

The fact that you are standing indicates you have more to accomplish. Use your valuable encounters wisely and exhibit great humility. You also possess the power to create change!

Contents

CHAPTER ONE

Light in Darkness

A life filled with great despair caused me to believe that I would not live past the age of twenty-one. Either someone would kill me because I wasn't worthy of living, or the cares of the world would weigh me down so heavily that I would self-destruct along the way. I didn't have hopes, dreams, or aspirations. I was merely surviving. Inhaling and exhaling oxygen, waiting for the day I met my maker. I invested all my faith and trust in people. I made it their responsibility to bring me happiness, but most times, they did just the opposite. I was emotionally, mentally and physically beaten down; I barely had the strength or will to survive. It was only by the grace of God that I am standing today. I am so very grateful that I am No Longer a Prisoner.

I always looked forward to Sleep and sometimes fantasized about it. Outside of the many nights that I had night terrors, going to sleep was one of the most enjoyable times of my life. It didn't matter what time of day it was or how long I had already slumbered; Sleep was my friend because it never made me feel worthless or anxious. While spending time with my friend, Sleep, I had a few brief moments of peace in a hopeless world. I felt free with no worries. I was able to relax.

Because I experienced extreme bullying for many years as a child, along with being in abusive relationships as a teen, the feeling of rejection was all too familiar. I didn't fit in, but so desperately wanted to. I thought that if someone killed me, the world would be better because of my death. The only people who would care about me being taken out would be my parents, my sisters and maybe one or two neighborhood friends. The concern of being murdered began in high school when a group of girls planned to jump me. One of the girls in the group approached me...

"You are making your deathbed," she said, flashing me a wicked smile.

"What do you mean?" I asked, trying desperately to hide the fear in my voice. This was a girl I hardly even knew so I wondered why she had an issue with me.

"What! You don't know?" The girl who was much bigger and stronger than I asked. I could hear the seriousness in her voice, and I blinked in confusion, trying to think of how I may have offended her.

"What...what...are you talking about?" I asked her again.

"You gonna' get taken out! Everyone is tired of you always talkin' shit," she said with a mocking smile.

I was more confused at this point. "What are you talking about?" I asked her again.

"Are you blind or just dumb? Everyone in school can't stand you, Wendy. You're corny!" She sounded so confident and assured that the only thing I wanted to do at that time was to run away. I didn't do that. I immediately recoiled into a shell.

This was something I never expected to hear in high school. I couldn't understand why people hated me to the point of speaking about taking me out. I never did anything to them. I barely knew them. Instead of believing the positive affirmations that my parents attempted to instill in me, I assumed something was wrong with me.

I must have deserved poor treatment. If I was as great as my parents exclaimed, people would not have constantly belittled me. After a while, I memorized their hurtful words which echoed in my mind day and night. I was called Pig Girl because of my full nose and was criticized because of my long, slender fingers. I hated the way I looked; I hated every part of me, inside and out. Their words of destruction and torment became a part of me. I believed that I was stupid and ugly. I hung on to their every harsh word. My parents always focused on the good in me, but I didn't. They believed that I was a special child and had always tried to shield my sisters and me from external forces.

"Mom, do you think I'm ugly?" I asked my mom one day. As soon as she heard my small quivering voice, she turned, smiled warmly at me and spread her arms for me. Like a child, I ran into her open arms, trying to feel protected.

"Why would you think that you're ugly?" she asked, still smiling at me.

"Well, Mom...I...I...," I stammered. The truth of the matter was that I didn't have the guts to tell her that I was being bullied in school. I simply accepted what was happening as my fate.

"Nee, is someone picking on you?" she asked me, searching my eyes for answers.

"No, Mom," I hastily shook my head.

My mom immediately pulled me into her loving arms for a full minute, never letting me go.

"Listen to me, sweetie," she finally said, releasing me and staring into my eyes.

"You are not an ugly girl. You are God's special creation. Your father and I love you very much and nothing will ever change that."

She stroked my smooth cheeks and seeing that I wasn't convinced, she pulled a stool and sat down, pulling me into her arms.

"You're beautiful, baby."

"Don't you think my fingers are too long?" I asked her. My mom merely stared at me, surprised I was suddenly asking her these questions.

"Nee Nee, your fingers are perfect."

"You think they are beautiful?" I wanted desperately to hang on to her every word.

"Yes, your hands are soft and delicate. You can be a great pianist one day." She kissed my fingers, trying to reassure me.

When I remained quiet, she smiled again and said, "Baby, your hands are dainty and feminine, just like you. One day, you'll grow up and appreciate having beautiful hands. God created you in His special image and likeness. "How could you possibly think that you are ugly?"

"Do you think my nose is...?" I began but my mom bent her legs and kissed my nose. "Your nose is beautiful; I would never lie to you." She smiled again.

I never believed what my mom said. I just thought that she said all those words to assure me. I thought since they were my parents, they had to say kind things because it was their job.

As a kid, I ate scrapple for breakfast and brought some in for the kids at school. The kids in my third-grade class loved it until I told them scrapple is pig scraps.

Before Mom would begin her bath, she lathered her legs with shaving cream, then shaved them from her ankles to her thighs. While on the school playground, I lathered my tiny, frail legs with Vaseline, then scraped the Vaseline off with the smooth side of a plastic knife. I wanted to do everything I witnessed my mother do.

After my scrapple episode, the kids in my class said they no longer wanted to be my friend. A group of them hung out after school and wrote a song about me. The lyrics are as follows:

They sang the song in unison as they all read from their own personal copies. They seemed to have really enjoyed singing a song about how horrible I was. While alone in my room that evening I began to sing the song too because if they said it maybe it was true. This song was created over twenty-eight years ago, yet I still can recite it verbatim.

I grew up in a loving two-parent home with my two sisters. My parents were active in our lives, which was another glimpse of peace in a hopeless world. As a family, we enjoyed barbecuing, bike riding and snowball fights. Although I received love, support and protection at home, it didn't seem to carry me through when out of my parent's sanctuary. The lies of destruction began to take root around the age of fifteen. I didn't fit in as a teen and at that time I wanted to, so I hung out with a group of girls from around the way. They claimed to be my friends, but most of them really weren't. One day, I was lying down on my couch by an open window when I heard noises. I suddenly woke up just to hear a group of girls plotting against me. One of which was someone who was just in my kitchen the day prior, eating a cake baked by my mom. "Wendy is gonna' get hers," I heard Dashawna say.

"I got her fooled... She think we cool so this is our perfect time," she said in a clear and loud voice.

"Are you sure this gonna' work?" I heard a girl whose voice I couldn't recognize say.

"She think we cool." Dashawna laughed.

"I'm gonna' ask her to come out, and when she do, we gonna' dump bleach on her and then jump her ass."

I heard giggles coming from the other girls. They obviously loved the idea of dumping bleach on me and beating me up.

"How you gonna' get her out the crib?" another girl had asked. "I'm gonna' see if she wanna' chill, and once she agrees, we will get her to a secluded area, jump her and let her know what time it is." Dashawna tried to persuade them.

"Let's do this," the other girls agreed.

"Go 'head and hide. Don't come out until I give you the signal."

I lay down, feeling miserable, and then I heard the girls laughing and clapping their hands. I had always thought that Dashawna was my friend, but I didn't know that I was simply making a fool out of myself.

Shortly after their conversation, my doorbell rang, and I ran to get it. I yanked it open and found Dashawna grinning at me with so much innocence.

"What up, Dashawna?" I greeted, forcing a smile on my face. "Hey Wendy, what up?" she smiled back at me, flashing me her teeth.

"Wanna come in?" I asked her, but deep down, I didn't want her anywhere near me.

"Nah, I wanna' see if you wanna' come out to chill." "Where?" I asked her, feigning ignorance.

"Let's go chill on the block," she replied.

Since I knew what was about to happen, I didn't dare go out with her. I simply sent her my best smile and then said, "I'm good, Dashawna; I'm about to just chill in the crib." I saw her face suddenly change and she looked frustrated.

"Nah, come chill?" she asked, trying to convince me. I grinned. "I'll catch ya later."

I saw her open her mouth as if to protest, but she suddenly changed her mind and shut it back.

"Peace," she said, not caring to hide the disappointment in her face. "Peace," I responded and slowly shut the door. Once the door was shut, I ran upstairs towards the window and peeped out.

"Girl what happened?" Ebony asked her.

"She said she stayin in the crib." Dashawna looked angry.

"Why you ain't get her to come out?" one of the girls asked Dashawna.

"I tried to, but there was no need. Wendy said she was stayin in the crib, and if I kept trying to press her, she would have known something was up. I just let it ride."

The girls smirked. "Wendy messed up our plan. We were supposed to beat that ass." Ebony sounded angry.

"Don't worry, Ebony; we gonna' get her sooner or

later. Don't forget that she still think we cool."

From my window, I watched the girls nod in agreement and slowly walk away. Only then did I realize Dashawna wasn't my friend at all.

Most times, I napped in my bedroom, but for some odd reason, I decided to nap by the open window that day. I woke up just in time to hear the conversation taking place outside my home. I sometimes wonder what would have happened if I had gone out with them that day. How would the chain of that event have impacted the story that I am sharing with you today?

High school was the toughest time in my journey. When I was in eighth grade, I heard about Freshman Friday, which was a day when the upperclassmen beat up freshmen. I heard they sometimes locked them in their lockers. The upperclassmen never really bothered me much, though, not even on days they were supposed to. I seemed to have gotten along better with older people. I'm sure having a sister whom most of them respected didn't hurt either. My older sister, Ros, was attractive, tough and popular. My girlfriends really wanted to hang out with her, and most of my little boyfriends had a secret crush on her, which they didn't think I knew about. Their faces lit up when she walked by. They would try to play it cool, but they didn't fool me. Ros never seemed to have to try to fit in; she just naturally did. I fantasized about being just like her one day.

While living in Palm Lakes, a group of girls came to my house wanting to fight me over a boy. The ex–girlfriend was mad about their breakup and his new interest in me, so she rallied five girls and came to my house to make trouble. As the voices outside my home became louder, I made my mother aware of what was taking place. My mother immediately told me to tell my older sister, who has always been my protector. My mom was also tough, which is where Ros got it from. As I was telling my mom that I didn't want to tell Ros because I was scared she would get beat up too, Ros had already put her sneakers on and was darting out the front door. I guess she automatically knew what was happening since girls always seemed to have a problem with me. I peeked through the curtain and witnessed my hero confront six girls with no fear. My mom stood at the front door out of sight. Ros said,

"If yawl have a problem with my sister, yawl have a problem with me!!!"

She placed her hands on her hips and rolled her neck. "If yawl came to fight her, you have to fight me first!" She also added a bunch of curse words. Every single one of them backed down. I was amazed! There were six of them and one of her, yet they quieted down and left the scene after being confronted by my hero. It was obvious they were all scared of her; of course, Ros looked fit and trimmed and she, unlike me, had succeeded in commanding a lot of respect from the kids in the neighborhood already.

When I had bad dreams, which was often, Ros would allow me to sleep in bed with her.

On the nights I experienced extreme night terrors, she would stay up all night rubbing my back until I felt safe enough to allow myself to fall asleep. My dreams were terrifying; I would literally stay up the entire night and most of the following morning. The terrors became so bad that my mom called the saints from the church. A group of them walked in, praying and anointing everything with Holy oil throughout the house, especially my bedroom.

They prayed with and for me. They told me that I had a calling on my life from God, which is the reason why the devil was after me at a young age. They said I would grow up to be a Mighty Warrior Of God. I was eight years old when my night terrors were the most extreme. Some nights, I would wake up trembling and remain trembling for several minutes before I could be made calm. I loved to be close to my sister. She always made me feel safe. Night terrors haunted me from about age four until my late-teens. I still have occasional bad dreams, but nothing like when I was a kid.

When Ros and I were teens she no longer allowed me to sleep in bed with her. I know you're probably thinking "a teen sleeping in bed with their sister… " Yep, I wanted to sleep in bed with her because those night terrors were vicious.

Before moving to Palm Lakes, I thought that haunted houses were only on TV, but the house that we lived in was a real one. When the entire family would be watching movies in our family room, we would all hear people running up and down the steps, but no one was there. Doors would close and open on their own and our basement had demonic writing on the walls. The entire house had a very eerie energy. Even my neighbors shared ghost stories about my house and the people who lived there prior to us.

Some nights, when the terrors were unbearable, after Ros fell asleep, I would quietly sneak into her room and make a bed on her floor with a few blankets and my pillow. I'm so grateful I outgrew night terrors because they were worse than any nightmare you could ever imagine.

The fear was so great that turning on every light in my house didn't offer comfort.

Most monsters disappear when you turn on the lights, but the monsters I was dealing with stayed, even if the lights were on or if it was broad daylight.

During the week, Mom and Dad dropped my little sister, Lisa, off at school while Ros left early to prepare for her track meets, leaving me in our house all alone. While getting ready for school, I turned on the radio and blasted Carter and Sanborn in the Morning on Power 99 FM. I loved when Horace the Taurus came on the air and said… "Keeeeep your head to the stars baby bubbles…. Whooooooo!!!!!!!!!" I also turned on every TV, hoping to create enough background noise to drown out the monsters calling my name. Some nights, I was woken out of my sleep just to see ghosts standing at the foot of my bed or in my closet. It's easy to think haunted houses only exist on TV until you live in one.

Growing up, Ros was my second mom. We had tons of fun making paper dolls, biking, swimming and playing at the playground in the second court. A few of our favorite toys were Lite-Brite, Easy Bake Oven and the Barbie dream house with the elevator.

We spent most of our childhood on a military base called McGuire Air Force Base, Falcon Courts North. It was a peaceful gated community where your neighbors were family.

In order to enter the community, one needed to have a military identity card or a special sticker on the upper right-hand corner of one's car. Dad would pull up, salute the gatekeeper, and wait to be waved in.

We never locked doors to our cars or homes; there was no need. We all trusted and respected one another.

My family got along with everyone, especially Millie and The Hurles. The Hurles' house was full of boys who loved rock and roll. My favorite song back then was I love Rock N Roll by Alan Merril. Mr. Hurles made stilts for all the neighborhood kids, and Memaw, the boys' grandmother, would watch my sisters and me when Mom and Dad had to work. Memaw took great care of us. I also had a friend named Chris Lane, who lived up the hill, with whom I remain in contact.

Each of my friends was different from me—whether it was their nationality, their native tongue, or the country in which they were born.

McGuire, AFB was a great place to grow up. Twenty-four hours a day, we would hear airplanes flying over our homes. These planes sometimes caused the house to shake. It was normal to see tanks, armed guards and military police patrolling the grounds.

Each section of our community consisted of courts and each court had a different playground. Down the hill from our house was where the high-ranking military officers lived. They gave out the best candy on Halloween. Nothing like receiving a full-size Snickers Bar or Reese's Cup! Sometimes they even gave us quarters which were enough to buy a couple pieces of candy from the mini-mart or a handful of Swedish Fish from 7-Eleven.

Our court, the first court, had a large swing set along with a large and small slide. The small slide had orange steps leading to the top, upon which we had a great time climbing. We would compare who arrived at the top first and then make fun about it. I especially enjoyed climbing the steps faster than my sister and everyone else. Ros and I used to flip over the bar at the top of the large slide before sliding down. Some of the smaller kids would pee down the slide or even make mud pies at the bottom, which was annoying but nothing a little rain couldn't wash away.

Ros and I swung so high on the swing set it felt like we were flying. Once we reached our highest peak on the swings we would jump off and compare who jumped the furthest.

The second court had large turquoise-blue and yellow monkey bars with fireman poles which we would climb up and slide down. Most times mom wanted us to stay in our court so she could look out the back door and watch over us while playing. If we were really good she would sometimes allow us to go to the second court to play. She would always tell us to take care of each other and since we promised we would, she trusted us to go to the next court.

Ros and I would wake up early and go out to play all day. Literally all day... We disliked playing indoors and didn't even want to go inside for lunch, snack, or to use the bathroom. While outside, we allowed our imagination to soar. I remember digging a large hole under the slide in our court because we were told that if we dug deep enough, we would reach China. My sister and I dug that hole day in and day out, excited about meeting Chinese people, but we never did. We also sang a special song on rainy days. The lyrics were: "Rain, rain, go away, come back another day..." We would sing until the rain stopped. There was so much to see and do outside.

On the days our rain song didn't work, we were forced to play inside, which we enjoyed the least but made the best of it. One of my favorite outdoor activities was bike riding at the schools. Our schools were located on large hills, a short walk from our house. We enjoyed riding our bikes down the big hills with our feet off the pedals while holding tightly to the handlebars to ensure we didn't fall. Sometimes we would ride with friends standing on the back pegs of the bike or we would ride with no hands which were the coolest of them all.

We played until it was dark, caught a few lightning bugs, and when the street lights came on, it was time to go inside. My mom would open the back door and shout, "Ros and Nee Nee, it's time to come in." We would reply by saying, "Coming, Mom," while running towards the sound of Mom's voice. We grew up in a strict yet very loving home.

When the side parking lot of our home would become icy in the winter months, Ros and I would run and slide across the patch of ice, pretending to be ice skaters. Mom would bundle us up so tightly that we could barely move. We would wear our snowsuits, boots, hats, scarves, and gloves. Mom would just about wrap our entire faces up with the scarf, which made it difficult to see. As long as we were warm, Mom was happy. When we returned from playing in the snow she would have hot chocolate waiting for us. I loved mine with marshmallows.

Ros and I had daily chores such as cleaning our rooms and washing the dishes. I had a cat, so I was also responsible for changing the litter box. I hated cleaning that stinkin' litter box. The box cleaning consisted of wearing large yellow gloves, which most people used for washing dishes, a plastic grocery bag, a little shovel and a water hose. My job was to dump the dirty litter in the plastic bag, scrape the waste stuck to the bottom into the same bag, spray the box with the water hose until clean and then add fresh litter. I cleaned the box properly for a while, then figured out a way to make it appear as if it were clean by simply dumping the dirty litter in a plastic bag and pour fresh litter on top. The halfway process worked for a while, but after some time, the fresh litter was no longer able to camouflage the waste chunks that stuck to the bottom. They were big and smelled really bad. I did, however, enjoy putting my doll's dresses on my cat, Kitty Shmuckahs. He was all black with white paws, a little white patch on his face and green eyes. I also used hair products in his hair and even managed to secure a barrette on the top of his head. He didn't mind wearing the dresses, but he didn't like wearing barrettes, so he would shake his head back and forth until the barrettes would fall out of his hair. He also didn't care for the Blue Magic grease that I used, so he would constantly lick his paws then rub his head with his wet paws to remove the product.

He loved riding in Lisa's baby stroller. I would pack a bag of treats, dress him up in either my doll's dress or a pair of Lisa's baby pants, and then off we went for a walk in the stroller.

After our walk, I would push Kitty Shmukahs on the swings and merry-go-round. At first, he was afraid of swinging and would try to jump out of my arms, but after a while, he would sit still and enjoy the ride. He was my best friend.

My siblings and I were raised to respect our elders and always respond with yes or no. Sometimes, depending on my dad's mood, we had to use the word sir or ma'am. Saying yea or what or having our elbows on our table while having family dinner was not acceptable.

Every Saturday was designated as cleaning day.

Mom would blast the radio, playing any song by Barry White, Luther, Teddy Pendergrass, The Mississippi Mass Choir or Patty through the house. My parents loved to sing and dance, but no matter how great the music or how great my parent's level of engagement was, I hated cleaning. The only thing I enjoyed about it was when it was over. I was able to watch Saturday Supercades, which was a jam-packed day filled with the best cartoons on the planet. It was a combination of all my favorite weekday cartoons, along with a few little extras. During the weekdays, while preparing to leave for school, I watched Jem, Alvin and the Chipmunks, The Jetsons and Jaba Jaws. After school, I enjoyed watching the Snorks and Fraggle Rock. Our after-dinner family shows were Little House on the Prairie, Three's Company, Sanford and Son, Good Times, The Jeffersons, What's Happening and All in the Family. Some days, I watched Small Wonder, which is about an engineer who created a robot and attempted to pass her off as his adopted daughter, Vici. The family worked hard to hide Vici's true identity and portray a normal life to the neighbors. I also loved to watch Wonder Years more than any other show. Winnie Cooper and Kevin Arnold were the power couple of the '80s!

Every weekend, Mom would watch The Color Purple on VHS. Sometimes, she would watch it multiple times a day. She watched it so much that I knew what Miss Celie, Shug Avery or Harpo was going to say and do next. Ros and I would do the Makidada hand clap before bed. Everyone in our family grew to love the movie just as much as Mom.

After dinner, Ros and I were permitted to have dessert if we ate all our food. We both hated our veggies, so we would smash our peas or succotash against the plate to make it appear as if we ate some of them. Not only was my sister tough, she was very clever. I learned all of my "get over on our parents' techniques" from her. Sometimes I hid my veggies in my mashed potatoes, threw a few on the floor under the table, or fed them to my cat. I would do anything to avoid eating them.

After my parents caught on, Ros figured out a way for us to have dessert without eating the food we hated. There was a ditch in our yard right next to our back door, which Ros used to dump our food. Of course, I had to give her some of my ice cream or snack to dump mine along with hers, but it was well worth it. Anytime we didn't like what our parents prepared for us, we would just dump it in the ditch. We got away with it for a while, and then my parents saw our little ditch filled with food, and we both got in trouble, so we had to come up with a new plan. Even though she didn't like her veggies, Ros would just eat them and be done with it in order to have dessert if she had to. She never made a big deal out of anything. She had a "go with the flow" type of attitude, even at a young age. Ros was always the first to finish her dinner, so she would be the first one to enjoy dessert. We both looked forward to dessert. One-night, Ros, Mom and Dad all finished their dinner well before me and went upstairs into Dad's den to hang out. I wanted to be upstairs with them, but I had to eat my dinner first.

I was a scaredy-cat and hated being alone, especially downstairs in the dining room. That night, Daddy made his special chocolate cake; I still had to eat my veggies before I could have some. I became tired of sitting in the dining room all alone while Ros had cake

and got to hang out with our parents, so I opened the
back door. It was pitch black outside, and I was afraid,
but I wanted that cake, so I quickly ran next door and
flung all of the food from my dinner plate into the
neighbor's backyard. After I dumped my plate, I ran
upstairs and told my parents I ate all my food. My
mom knew my track record of hiding or throwing away
food, so she checked the trash and found it empty. She
checked my little food ditch and found that empty too.
Finally, I could have some chocolate cake! I was happy!
I was able to join the party! I enjoyed hanging out in
the den with my family while listening to Heat Wave,
Al Green and The Temptations. We danced and laughed
the night away in Daddy's special den!!

Dad's dance moves consisted of bending his knees
up and down while spreading his arms in a flying motion.
He looked so funny! My dad was very artistic and loved
to draw. The walls of the den were covered in old record
albums ranging from The Blackbyrds, Aretha Franklin,
Four Tops, Diana Ross, Smokey Robinson and Tina Marie.
He relaxed in his red leather chair as he drew pictures
of his favorite artists. The next morning, our neighbor,
Dave, told my mom that someone dumped food in his
backyard. Mom looked at me and knew I was the culprit
by the look on my face.

"Nee Nee, why did you do it?" Mom asked me.

I looked down at my toes guiltily but said not a
word. "I am talking to you," my mom said, clearly
disappointed.

"Mom, Dad, last night I wanted to be with you
guys, but I couldn't because I didn't finish my dinner," I
fessed up, feeling guiltier.

"Continue speaking," my dad's voice was so sharp

that I shuddered.

"I...I also wanted to have cake for dessert, but since I can't do that unless I finish my food, I..." At this point, I fell silent, but then, when my mom looked sharply at me, I swallowed and continued speaking. "I wanted chocolate cake, so I threw my food in Mr. Dave's yard." I looked down again. "Now, Nee Nee, Apologize to Mr. David," my mom said.

I looked up into the man's eyes and said, "I'm sorry Mr. David."

The man merely nodded and walked away.

"You're going to be punished for this," my dad promised me.

I was placed on punishment. I couldn't go outside for the entire day because of what I did. I was miserable not being able to play outdoors with Ros. I couldn't use our food ditch, and I couldn't dump the food I didn't like in the neighbor's yard; so many nights, I just sat at the table, refusing to eat until I fell asleep. Peas, succotash and spam were horrible to eat. No matter how much ketchup, cheese or bread I added, it was still the worst meal on the planet. I would rather not eat than eat that. If I didn't like what mom or dad prepared, I wouldn't eat at all. Mom said that I ate like a bird and was very picky. Sitting at the table all night, all alone, was better than eating some of the food that was placed on our dinner table. After many nights of falling asleep at the table, my parents compromised. If I ate a small portion of my veggies, I would be excused from the table and still be able to have dessert. I was happy with the compromise, so I ate a spoonful of veggies in order to be dismissed.

When Ros and I became teenagers, she seemed

like she couldn't stand me sometimes, and I got on her nerves, but I guess that was normal because, through it all, she was always there when I needed her most. I have the best older sister anyone could ever have. My little sister isn't too shabby either. Lisa and I are five years apart, so when I was hanging out with Ros, Lisa was in Pampers. Lisa and my dad were inseparable. My mom made a little doll of my dad named Header Doll, which accompanied Lisa everywhere because she couldn't stand to be away from him. Lisa and I didn't hang out much as children, but now share many fond memories as adults. I love you very much, Risa Face and Rozy Boz!

My dad was as sharp as a tack. In leisure or business, he invested a great deal of time in his appearance. He took great pride in being in the Air Force. He shined his shoes so thoroughly that you could literally see your reflection in the toe of his boot. He had one large brush, a toothbrush and a rag for shining. He placed his large black brush into the polish, spit on the toe of his boot and would shine those shoes for hours. He used Niagara Starch to crease his pants. The creases were so crisp that they would cut you.

When not working, Dad loved to play spades, have friends over and play basketball. He kept a fresh pair of next-season Nikes under his bed each year. When his friends would come over, they would crowd around the dining room table. The downstairs filled with cigarette smoke while the grownups sipped their drinks, blasting The Temptations, and partied. Dad would shout, "Baby needs a new pair of shoes," and have me blow the dice. He said that when I blew the dice it made him win. All my parents' friends had children, so when our parents partied on the weekend, we would sneak snacks, play hide and seek, and get into anything that we knew we weren't supposed to. Our parents were so busy having fun that they said yes to just about anything. Perfect example, I usually was only allowed to have one piece of cake for dessert. If mom and dad were partying I would ask for cake multiple times and they would say yes to get me out of their hair. The grownups would party all night, which meant we didn't have a bedtime. Sometimes, they would even lose track of time and forget to make sure we had our baths. Half the time, we only played in the water anyway. When the grownups partied, so did we.

Not being a stranger to hard work, dad worked multiple jobs just to make ends meet. While being enlisted in the Air Force he also painted houses with his friend, Greene, for extra cash.

I never once heard my father complain. No matter what battle came our way; daddy was always up to the challenge. Being raised in a family with limited resources I learned that there is nothing more valuable than having a family who loves you. If you don't have a lot of money but you are loved, clean and have food to eat, you have all that you need.

My mom secured her first job at Roy Rogers in Wrightstown, New Jersey to help with bills. We celebrated her first job as a married woman. It was hard, at first, being without my mom during the day because she was the person I woke up to and hung out with all day. Mom gave me Daddy's sweater to change into while watching Mr. Rogers. She also gave me Daddy's red FMS hat to wear when I was pretending to be a firefighter while watching Sesame Street.

Daddy noticed that I was withdrawn and down

after Mom went to work, so he said that it was time to hit the road. Dad, Ros and I took a ride through Roy Rogers drive-through. I anxiously waited in a long line of cars ahead of us. Dad pulled up to the speaker to place our order, and I heard my mom's voice! I was excited that my mom worked at Roy Rogers; she sounded so cool taking our order through the microphone. When my dad pulled up to the window to collect our food, we were welcomed by mom! She was standing at the window with the biggest smile on her face, holding our bags of food. Not only did I get to hear her voice, I was able to see her. My mom was so beautiful (still is) and full of life. After seeing Mom, I wasn't sad anymore. We parked in the lot across from our house. After parking, Dad said, "Last one home is a rotten egg!" Ros, Dad, and I laughed while dashing to our front door as quickly as we could. Ros always won, and I was always the rotten egg. However, I was a happy rotten egg because I enjoyed being with my family. I counted down until Mom returned. Daddy kept us busy playing games. Before I knew it, Mom was home to help Dad tuck me in.

When I was told to keep a secret, I promised I would. I had every intention to, but something always made me tell. I could never help but to spill the beans... One evening Mom drove the car to work and left us home with Dad. He took two empty glass Budweiser bottles and filled them with apple juice. Dad and Ros both told me to pretend that we were drunk when Mom walked in the door. Right before she walked in Dad put Ros on one of his knees and me on the other. He sat down in his chair directly in front of the door to our home. Dad had his beer in one hand and Ros and I were holding our fake beer. When Mom walked in the door I pretended to be drunk and told her that daddy gave us beer. My mom flipped! She screamed to the top of her lungs,

"Eddie, you have my girls drinking beer!" "What did you do!"

"What's wrong with you?"

Dad and Ros started to laugh. I was startled to see my mom so upset for the first time, so I quickly hopped from my dad's lap and ran to my mom and said, "Mommy, it's just apple juice... we were just playing."

I looked back at my dad, and he smirked and said, "Nee Nee spilled the beans again."

Mom had merely smiled and then kissed my dad on the lips. Once everything settled, we all laughed and enjoyed the rest of our night. My childhood was really great. I had loving and caring parents, a protective older sister and an adorable younger sister. I didn't understand what happened to change everything when I grew into a teen. I suddenly lost my confidence, my sense of humor and my laughter.

CHAPTER TWO

Fresh out the Gate

I called our family car the Blue Bomber because it looked like the red, white and blue Bomb Pop you get from the ice cream truck. It was turquoise, with pink rust at the bottom around the wheels. Although I ducked down in my car while driving past my friends, I realized that it was what we could afford, and as Mom used to say, it got us from point A to point B. The Blue Bomber transported many blankets and food to the homeless in New York and Philly during our church trips and outings. My family and I attended church three days a week for what felt like ten hours for each gathering.

"Why do we have to go to church three times a week?" I often wondered, but my mom was focused on ensuring that everyone in our household became saved.

"We all need to communicate with Jesus and thank Him for all He has been doing in our lives," Mom would say. "But Adelia's parents don't make them go to church three times a week." At that time, I didn't understand why we seemed so different when it came to church. "Come on Nee Nee, God is good," Mom would say and then pull me into her embrace. As a kid, I didn't realize that the foundation was being built, but as I look back, I am grateful that I got to know Christ at the young age of eight. Mom continued working at Roy Rogers while Dad worked multiple jobs to save for a new car. We made a huge upgrade by going from the Blue Bomber to a new, dark blue Chevrolet Caprice Classic wagon with wood siding, which was my favorite car as a kid. On large family trips, we would pile up in the back and sit on laps if necessary. Wearing seatbelts was not the law back then. Those were the days...

I grew up on the military base most of my childhood, but at the age of fourteen, Dad retired, and I was forced to live a civilian life. Living outside of my gated community felt like a whole new, less exciting, scary world. I no longer felt a sense of family and camaraderie. I literally felt like I was going into shock outside of the security of "the gate!" On my first day of junior high in the civilian world, a group of girls bullied me. I was fresh off McGuire and very naive to how different their world was from what I was used to. I expected everyone to be kind and respectful, just like all my old friends. My dad walked me into my new middle school because I was too nervous to enter the building alone.

"Do you think I will make new friends?" I asked Dad, staring into his loving eyes.

Dad smiled at me. He pulled me into his embrace and affectionately patted the top of my head. "Who wouldn't want to be friends with Nee Nee?" he asked, looking baffled.

"But Dad, I just thought that since..." Dad wouldn't let me complete my sentence. He silenced me by placing his finger on his lips.

"Shhhh," he grinned, and I found myself grinning back. "I can't imagine anyone not wanting to be your friend," Dad said, sounding so confident. I believed him. He reassured me that everything would be okay as I shared my fear of having to start all over and make new friends. He walked me to my homeroom and then turned around to exit the building. As soon as he was halfway down the hall, away from me, a girl who was at her locker looked back at me, rolled her eyes and said, "I heard you were messing with my boyfriend."

I wanted so desperately to scream for my dad, but I was in middle school; I just couldn't do that! It was bad enough that he walked me into the building. I guess she sensed that I wasn't from the area and was a little nervous by the way I looked around, confirming that I was truly out of my element.

"My dad just retired from the military, we just moved here," I replied.

The girl stared at me as if I was insane. She had a small smile on her lips as she looked me up and down. When she said nothing more, I swallowed, feeling more nervous.

"I don't know your boyfriend. You must be confusing me with another girl."

She and another girl came closer to me, invading my personal space.

"We don't like you!" the two girls said, looking disdainfully at me.

I was puzzled. It was my first day of school... how could people dislike me after only being in the building for ten minutes? A teacher yelled for us to get to class, and we all dispersed. The entire day, I couldn't focus on school because I was so occupied with how I was treated within the first few minutes of being in the building. I didn't expect such a high level of unwanted stress and drama on my first day, especially when I didn't know anyone to make enemies with.

In eighth grade, we boarded our bus for our science class field trip. I typically kept to myself in science class because I sensed that many of the girls who claimed to be my friends didn't really like me. I've had a strong discernment of people and things since I was very young, and I've learned to always trust my gut, especially because it has been right one hundred percent of the time. I can pick up on the true intentions of those around me. At times, I felt like it was a blessing and a curse. It was a blessing because I knew who to stay away from or who not to share all of me with. Yet it felt like a curse because I witnessed how unauthentic many people are. Sometimes, it felt easier to try to allow myself to be fooled by their empty words and fake smiles. It felt less painful and easier to cope with. Being able to see past big smiles and kind words prompted me to test my theory. I wanted to be wrong since the girls in my class were always so kind and helpful. I even had lunch with them and talked to them on the phone after school. If I observed their actions alone, I would have believed they had positive intentions of me, but my gut told me otherwise, so I had to get clarity and confirmation.

On the bus, I sat alone, one seat in front of them even though I was invited to join them in the back of the bus. The kids loved to sit in the back of the bus because we were further away from the bus driver, which offered more time to goof off. The back seat also allowed us to feel the hills and bumps more through the seats which made the bus ride feel more like a roller coaster.

I grabbed my Sony Walkman from my bag, put my headphones on and pretended to press play. I had to be convincing, so I bobbed my head to the pretend music, which was not actually playing. I also pretended to sing along to a song. I knew that I would be able to confirm or deny my theory if I could make them comfortable enough to display their true colors. While I was pretending to listen to music, they called my name to see if I could hear them. I was in fact, able to hear them, but pretended that I couldn't. After a few minutes of pretending to be listening to music, I fooled them into believing that I wasn't aware of what was actually taking place.

"I really can't stand Wendy anymore," I heard Darcy say. "She think she all that and a bag of chips... I can't stand her ass," Keisha said in contempt. "She ain't cute!" Kenya replied.

As the three girls conversed, I pretended to be busy with my music, but every word was like a blow to me.

"I don't like her hair. It's nappy," Keisha said. She reached out and touched a strand of my hair as if she was removing dirt from it. I turned, smiled at her and she smiled back, revealing a perfect set of small white teeth.

"She ugly," Kenya said.

"Wendy is so ugly I wonder where she came from," Darcy agreed. As they talked, I fought the urge to dig my hands into my pocket and remove the small mirror I had taken from Ros. My parents think I am so beautiful, and they dote on me, while my sister Ros was simply the best big sister I had. I tried to understand why these girls think I am ugly and not fun to be with.

"She wanna' be friends with us, but don't she know we don't want her to be one of us?" I heard Kenya say.

"She gon get hers, don't worry," Darcy said. At this point, I almost froze.

"You right, girl," Keisha groaned.

"Her fingers look like ol' lady skeletons," said Darcy.

"There ain't nothin' good about her," Kenya said disgustingly. "Darcy, your birthday coming up next week, you gonna' invite ugly Wendy?" I heard them speak and I held my breath, feeling hurt.

"No way! I ain't inviting Wendy. She'll mess up my party?" Darcy replied.

I looked back and smiled at them while they were speaking poorly of me, still pretending to be listening to music. After their words became unbearable, I removed my headphones, looked at them and smiled again; they smiled back.

"What are you listening to, Wendy?" Darcy asked, smiling sweetly at me.

"Cypress Hill," I replied, also smiling at the girls. I didn't behave like I heard all the ugly things they had spoken about me.

"Your hair is nice, I like the curls," Kenya retorted, her face masking her contempt of me.

"Thank you," I retorted, also smiling at the girls.

"I love your dress, girl; you look like a princess in it," Keisha smirked at me with a laugh on her face.

"My mom got it for me. I love it, but thanks, by the way." I smiled again, revealing my teeth to them. They said other playful words as if they never shared how much they couldn't stand me. I quietly sat alone, trying to process the confirmation of my theory. I never shared what I discovered. I kept their actions in the back of my mind, knowing they weren't who they claimed to be. I've learned to always trust my gut. Regardless of what anyone says or thinks. Heightened discernment is needed in a deceptive world.

The focus of high school was being pretty, athletic, popular or having sex. Most of us didn't think much about our future. I never envisioned being where I am today. I figured the hell I experienced in high school would last a lifetime. The girls were built like grown women, and then there was me. I looked so underdeveloped compared to the other girls my age. They had boobs, hips, and butts, and compared to them, I looked like a little runt. I was very petite, flat chested, about 4'9" and ninety-seven pounds soaking wet. I was usually the shortest and skinniest, even while standing next to kids a few years younger than me.

While the kids in high school were having sex, I was still fighting the urge to play with my Barbies. I never understood why I was so different. I hated it! They were more into boys than I was, which made me feel even more like something had to have been wrong with me. I liked boys, had boyfriends, but having sex was far from my mind. Seventh grade was when kids claimed to be in serious relationships. If you were a virgin, you were made fun of. A virgin in high school was unheard of! I wish I knew the value of being a virgin back then because if I did, I would have waited for my husband. No matter how many times my mom told me being a virgin was the most valuable treasure a girl could have, I still felt like I was missing out by not having sex at an early age like all the other girls. All my friends started having sex around age eight when I lived on McGuire. I felt like I was way behind. By high school, there were very few virgins, and most, like me, never announced it.

I worked during the summer babysitting for my aunt and uncle in West Chester, Pennsylvania. At the end of the summer, I took the money that I earned and went school shopping. I was not looking forward to going back to school with the girls who hated me, but I was feeling pretty good about the outfits I purchased. Right before school, I went and had my Jheri curl touched up at Marty's Salon, uptown, right around the corner of my aunt and uncle's house. Marty is a longtime family friend who took great care of all our hair. Even to this day, he is the only person my mom and aunt will allow to do their hair. I thought a fresh touch-up made my hair look silky, even though I didn't like the smell of the chemicals and moisturizers.

On my first day of ninth grade, I wore a pair of colorful stretch pants with a colorful baby doll shirt to match, along with some black flats with huge black bows on the top. The shirt had a large black collar, was fitted throughout my entire body, and then flared out around my waist. It was burgundy, gold, blue, black, purple and green. At the time of purchase, I didn't realize that it highlighted just how flat my chest was. I stared at girls' boobs, looking forward to the day when mine would become fuller. To me, my clothes looked happy but compared to all the other girls I looked like a baby wearing baby clothes. Needless to say, that was the first and last time I wore that outfit to school. Many of the kids who taunted me in middle school followed me to high school.

My mom told me that things would get better in high school, but things became a lot worse than I expected. I wasn't a troublemaker, but trouble seemed to find me. The girls who didn't like me came up with any and every reason to fight me. They approached me in packs like wolves and said things like, "I heard you were talking about me," or, "I heard you called me a bitch." I now know that those words meant they were jealous. Perhaps they had seen the greatness in me before I did?

As long as I can remember, my mom told me that people picked on me because I had many great qualities, and they were envious. I never saw the value in myself to understand why anyone would ever be envious of me. Each day, I dealt with someone lying on me, wanting to fight me, or making fun of my hair.

While at the lunch table in ninth grade, a short, dark-skinned girl asked me if I had a Jheri Curl, which is a permed curl patterned hairstyle that was popular in the African American community in the 80's. To maintain the curl pattern, a liquid activator had to be used on a regular basis. The activator had a horrible smell and left a residue on clothing and furniture. A Wave Nouveau is very similar to the Jheri Curl, but it requires less maintenance. The activator is a cream or gel versus a spray moisturizer, but they pretty much look the same. Those who wore Wave Nouveau didn't lose cool points, but those with Jheri curls were considered uncool in the early 90's. The girl at my lunch table, let's call her Ms. Jheri, confirmed that no one knew the difference. If they did, she would have never asked me whether my hair was processed with a Jheri Curl or Wave Nouveau. We didn't have expert stylists in our school; we were just a bunch of kids. Ms. Jheri claimed to have a Wave Nouveau, but her hair looked exactly like mine, wet and stringy with the same stinky Jheri Curl smell. As she asked me about my hair type, a crowd began to form around us. As the crowd became larger, she became louder. The moment of truth arrived; I had an opportunity to lie about my hair and be accepted or tell the truth and get picked on more. Most people in my situation would have chosen to say they had a Wave Nouveau just to fit in or be accepted. The thought of lying to fit in did cross my mind, but I chose to say I had a Jheri Curl. As much as I hated being picked on, I didn't want to lie to be accepted by anyone.

Whatever additional turmoil I was going to face because of my hair choice was something I would accept. The kids made fun of me the entire lunch period. They called me "drip drip, Jheri Curl" as they pranced around the table, I was sitting at. They all laughed as I remained seated, trying my best to ignore them. I didn't say anything back; I didn't defend myself. I felt that if the kids at my table were taunting me, maybe I deserved it. When the bell rang, I darted out of the lunchroom and proceeded to my next class.

I got along with all the boys and all the light-skinned, white, Spanish, or mixed girls. For some reason, the dark-skinned girls seemed to hate me. I was bullied from my very first day of middle school and throughout high school, which is where my greatest bully experience occurred.

Cheryl and I started out as friends. We had English class together and would clown around most of class. She was a true jokester and had a nonchalant attitude about everything. Putting us both in the back of the class together made for lots of laughs, ignoring our teacher and distracting the other students. On Wednesday, after class, I saw Cheryl hanging out at her lockers, so I approached her to hang out in the hall before our next class. As we were leaning against her locker, chatting about how much we couldn't stand class, a group of her friends approached us. She then stopped laughing with me and said she wanted to fight me. I was puzzled. I thought we were friends?

"What up?" I asked her, looking rather confused at the sudden change in her.

"Girl, please... You wanna' fight?" She looked very serious.

"Weren't we just buggin' out a few minutes ago?" I

asked her, looking from her to her friends.

"You gonna' lie to my face?" She asked me, looking very angry. I wondered what happened to make her transform like this. A few minutes ago, we were laughing and having fun and then suddenly, on sighting her friends, she transformed.

"What are you talking about?" I asked her again. "Don't try to lie... I heard what you did," she said, pointing her middle finger at me and angrily gritting her teeth.

"What did you hear?" I was still baffled by her sudden change in behavior.

"You gonna' deny the fact that you were talking about me behind my back?" she asked, still staring angrily at me.

"I'm gonna' deny it because I didn't say nothin' about you," I said, putting my hands on my small waist.

At that moment as I stood facing her and her group of friends, I realized that she was never my friend to begin with. I wasn't scared of her but was afraid of getting jumped. She and her crew were known for jumping people. They never fought one on one. The bell rang, and we all hurried to class. I was saved by the bell this time, but I knew they would come for me soon.

Cheryl and I were back in class the next day, and she didn't say a word to me, nor did I say a word to her. It was kind of quiet in the back of the classroom without anyone to joke with, but I let it be. Since I didn't have her to goof off with, I daydreamed during the entire period. I was still a bit confused by how she had pretended to be my friend since the first day of school but suddenly shifted because she "heard" I was talking about her.

The bell rang, and I immediately grabbed my books to quickly move to my next class to avoid getting jumped. Dipping and dodging to avoid getting jumped was overwhelming. I stopped going to my locker in between classes because the longer I was in the hallways, the greater the chance of me getting jumped. I started carrying most of my heavy textbooks in my backpack and arms throughout the day. I was on the small side and on top of that, I feared being jumped. The backpack alone caused me to tire easily. While other students in high school moved from class to class lightly, I had to deal with holding textbooks in my backpack and my arms. I didn't care about the back pain caused by the weight of my books; all I cared about was not getting jumped by Cheryl and her crew. My strategy of carrying all my books for the day had initially worked well for me, but I soon found myself becoming too exhausted from carrying everything in my backpack and arms. On days when I felt too tired to manage all my books, I decided to leave them in my locker, but this resulted in me being marked unprepared for class. Although losing points for not having my books was frustrating, it felt preferable to facing the risk of getting jumped. I didn't put in much effort while I was in school. I hardly paid attention.

I just daydreamed of how I would escape the mob of girls after me. I planned my safety route every day. Instead of focusing on the lesson, I had to map out a route to get to all my classes and get to the bus without getting beaten up. If I moved quickly enough between classes, I would make it home in one piece.

Before any planned fight, the girls would apply Vaseline to their faces to avoid getting bruised or cut. They would also carry large key chains, socks filled with large batteries, or roll in clicks. In my school, no one fought fair, which is the reason why I was so uncomfortable. I knew that if a bunch of girls jumped on me to beat me up, I would probably die. They already told me I was "making my deathbed" early on in my high school career, and on top of that, I was half their size. My life became a test of survival. As much as I hated my life, I didn't want to die from getting jumped. At my military schools, no one jumped people or carried weapons. If someone didn't like you or if you didn't like them, the fight would be you against them, not you against them, their grown cousins, sisters and friends.

I've been in fights before and was never afraid to fight until I got to Flopper High. From the very beginning of my freshman year all the way to the end, I was tormented by the girls from the other side of the track. I wasn't totally friendless, but because I chose to focus on everyone who didn't like me over those who did, it made the negative situation larger than it had to be. At Flopper, I ranked smack dab in the middle of the cool chart. I wasn't considered a nerd. Although looking back, the nerds were the coolest and smartest in my eyes. They knew that high school was only a microscopic part of their lives. As for me, high school was the hell that I never thought I would become free from. The kids, often labeled as nerds, were well-mannered, studied diligently, and had plans for their future after high school. They discussed their aspirations of attending college, participated in various school clubs, and had numerous colleges to choose from. Some even talked about the possibility of becoming foreign exchange students, which I had only seen on TV. I never thought about college or beyond. I was too busy just trying to stay alive. I didn't value myself as much as I should have, but I realized that an easy way to become popular overnight would be to date someone two grades above me. If he had his own car, that would be an even bigger bonus. The older guys seemed to be interested in me, and I was frequently asked out by boys from all grade levels, especially those who were much older. However, I always turned them down. I knew that if I dated an older guy, I would, in fact, become instantly popular, but sex was an expectation and I wasn't ready for all that. I had enough on my mind regarding survival... I didn't want to also have to think about having sex. Every second of Flopper became more difficult. Half the time, I would pretend to be sick just to avoid going to that hell hole.

Shona peeked in my classroom to see if I was there. I noticed the thick layer of Vaseline on her face while she was holding a large keychain. I knew what that meant. She was also wearing a long coat, which indicated that she may have been concealing weapons. I knew that once the bell rang, I would have to fight, but I was frightened because I knew it wouldn't be one-on-one. As soon as I heard the bell, I became more alarmed. Shona was peeking on the side of the door, waiting for me to come out. I wasn't sure who else was with her. I had to think fast; I didn't want to die. I approached my teacher and pretended to care about my grades.

"Miss Davis?" I asked her that afternoon.

Miss Davis looked up from the stalk of books before her and gave me a warm smile. "How can I help you, Wendy?" she asked me.

"My grades are barely passing, and I was wondering if I can make higher grades." I spoke; I allowed my gaze to touch the doorway. I found Shona frowning at me, obviously not happy with my new tactics.

"Of course, you can do better and earn higher grades if you study harder," she said while smiling.

"I want to do better in school and was hoping that you could help me."

Miss Davis looked up at me for a full minute. She was so thrilled about my perceived interest that she didn't realize I was stalling. Her thrill of me giving a crap about her class prevented her from noticing how distracted I was and that most of my attention was towards the door where Shona was peaking in. I couldn't care less about grades! I was just trying to survive!

The second bell rang, which meant that everyone should have been in their next class. I looked out the door and Shona was gone.

"Oh no!" I exclaimed, looking a bit worried.

"What is the problem?" Miss Davis asked me, looking worriedly at me.

"The second bell just rang, and I am still here. I had totally forgotten the time," I told her in a pretentious tone. She sighed in relief when she realized I was merely upset about being late for my next class. "Don't worry dear, I'll give you a late pass to give to your next teacher."

I smiled happily at her.

"Oh, thank you, Miss. Davis." I smiled again as she scrapped some notes on a piece of paper.

"Here you are." She handed the late pass and I excitedly stared at it. I walked out of the class, knowing I had succeeded in avoiding Shona and her friends this time, but I didn't know how long I could continue to avoid them. I had a few more classes to navigate before I would dart to my bus in order to get to the safe zone, which was home. I finished the next class and had one final class to go. I managed to survive both classes. The end of day bell rang, and the race began all over again. While students were going to their lockers to drop off the books they no longer needed and pick up items or homework to take home, I was darting to the school bus. Whatever was in my locker was going to stay there that day. I survived my day! I didn't get jumped; I didn't get beaten up and didn't get killed. I made it to my bus but still felt tense until it pulled off because the girls from the other side of the track were also known for trying to ride your bus and then jumping you when you got off. So glad my bus driver was on top of things like that. If you didn't have a note from your parents, you couldn't ride my bus.

On the bus ride home, everyone laughed, chit-chatted and shared about their day. They all seemed so relaxed and happy, without a care in the world. I, on the other hand, had no time to rejoice because I would be back to school the next day, planning my survival.

All the dodging and running became too much for me. My backpack was ripping from the weight of too many books being shoved in it, so I had to leave them in my locker. My teacher said that if I continued to arrive unprepared for class, I would have to stay for detention. I dreaded detention because that was where my bullies spent most of their time. I was tired of balling up my coat and putting it in my backpack. There was no other way out of this situation. I had to stop at my locker. I practiced my combo in my mind while speed-walking to my locker. I planned to quickly unload my first session books and load up the books for the remainder of the day. I had to move fast. In and out was always my strategy. Yes!!! It worked. I managed to drop off the books I didn't need and load up on the books I needed for the remainder of the day. I moved fast and was able to avoid the girls from the other side of the track. I was feeling confident but I knew I had to stop one more time before going home because if I didn't, I would get detention. I planned the same strategy—practice my combo in my mind, speed- walk down the hall, drop off my books and grab the books I placed on the top shelf of my locker. I did it once, and I was hoping to do it again. I was so focused on entering my combo I didn't see Cheryl come up from behind me. She walked towards me, yelling and screaming about how she was going to kick my ass for talking shit about her.

"Wendy, I'm gonna' kick your ass for talking shit about me... you gon' learn not to talk shit no more!!"

Hearing her, I immediately froze, wondering what I would do and how I would escape them this time. I was panicking. My heart began to race.

The louder she became, the more kids crowded around us. Before I knew it, I was surrounded by girls on every side of me. I was in a large circle. It felt intimidating to be surrounded by so many girls who wanted to hurt me. Ms. Jheri approached me and said, "You're making your deathbed." They finally caught up to me! I couldn't run any longer. I was about to die. While standing directly in front of me, Ms. Jheri turned to Cheryl and said, "Wendy has been talking shit about you; I heard her." I looked at Ms. Jheri and tried to understand why she hated me so much she would lie just to get crap started. I stared at her again, and then, I spoke.

"Cheryl, I never said anything about you."

"Are you calling me a liar?" Ms. Jheri asked, taking

a step toward me.

"Why would I tell you shit behind Cheryl's back when we ain't even cool and I don't even talk to you?" I asked her, trying to clear my name. The entire place suddenly became so quiet I could hear my heartbeat. I thought this day would be my last. The girls who didn't like me were there along with about seven girls from the other side of the track. A teacher came out of the classroom. "What are you kids doing outside your classrooms?" she asked us. No one dared to say anything to the teacher.

"Now, I want you all to return to your various classrooms or you will find yourselves in trouble," she threatened. The crowd dispersed, and my day continued. I let out a sigh of relief, silently thanking God for sending that teacher in the nick of time. I closed my eyes and shuddered at the thought of what would have happened to me if the teacher had not shown up. The next period was okay; I didn't have to fight, no one made fun of me, and no one bullied me. Towards the end of class, I started my regular countdown and strategy before I had to go home. Someone in class told me that I was going to get jumped after class, so I asked my teacher if I could use the bathroom. After I used the bathroom, I paced back and forth, trying to strategize. How was I going to survive this time? I told my parents what was going on, and they came to the school on multiple occasions. We met with the principal and the guidance department yet there was no relief. The school's response was they cannot act upon a rumor and if no one put their hands on me then I'll be fine. They also said they were thinking about installing metal detectors as if that would give us peace of mind. If anything, it made school feel even scarier. I felt as though I was in a school like the one in the movie 'Lean on Me,' but without Mr. Clark to save the day. Instead of returning to class, I walked through the halls, peeking in classrooms trying to find someone with a car. Finally, I saw my neighbor, who was a nice guy from Africa. He was kind of quiet and very respectful. I stood outside of his class and flagged him to come out. I was desperate; they were about to kill me, and no one was around to protect me. I didn't know what to do. When he came out of his class, I informed him about what was happening.

"A girl named Cheryl thought that I talked shit behind her back, and I didn't. Now she and her crew wanna' jump me!" I told him in a desperate tone, and he had listened very attentively to me, not even asking me questions. When I was through explaining, I swallowed, realizing the time had come for me to make a request.

"Can you take me home?" I asked him, looking very helpless and scared at the same time. "I'm so sorry, Wendy," he began, looking at me with concern.

"I can't leave school early because I have a couple of things to do." Hearing him say that, my heart sank, but then, I heard him continue talking. "How about I take you home after school?" he offered.

I had no issues with anyone on my bus; they were all neighborhood kids who all seemed to like me. I didn't know if I would survive long enough to make it to the bus. I frantically left his presence to plan my next strategy. After he went into his classroom, I decided to take a trip to the guidance office. I told them that it was an emergency and I needed to speak to someone right away. They sent a staff member to get my belongings from my class while I explained what was going on. It was considered snitching if you told your parents or teachers anything, but I didn't care. If someone was going to kill me, I needed to let someone know, so I did. I shared my issues with my guidance counselor without saying any names.

"I'm about to be killed," I told the man, looking very scared.

The guidance counselor merely looked at my scared face and immediately went on his feet. "What is your name kid?" he asked me.

"Wendy," I nervously responded.

He walked to me and placed his flat palms on my forehead and cheeks to ascertain that I wasn't running a temperature. I saw him sigh in relief when he saw that I was not ill.

"Who wants to kill you?" he asked me, offering me a seat.

"They want to kill me." I looked so frantic, but I didn't care.

He responded by saying, "Did anyone attempt to kill you?"

I shared about what Ms. Jheri said about me making my deathbed.

"That doesn't mean that they are going to kill you," he told me.

"Unless someone attempted to do you physical harm there is nothing we can do about it," he further explained to me.

I shared the incident that happened when I was surrounded in the hall.

"No one actually hit you, Wendy; trust me, you'll be fine." He tried to make me feel better. I reiterated the threats about "my deathbed and getting jumped."

"Unless someone puts their hands on you, there is nothing the school can do."

The expression on my face was one of sheer terror. The man smiled affectionately at me and then said, "If it continues, you should return to my office."

I slowly went on my feet and walked out of the office. The bullying continued, so my trips to guidance continued every other day. It became my new strategy. When I knew something was going to pop off, I would go to the guidance office. I even had lunch there from time to time. Going to the guidance office became a part of my routine. I never cared much about school anyway, so I wasn't concerned about missing class. Dodging bullies became my full-time job. Doing just enough to pass to the next grade and stay alive was all I needed to worry about. I had the potential to be a straight "A" student, but I barely tried, which resulted in averaging C's or D's. I received a few F's, but it was never enough to prevent me from moving on to the next grade. Besides, Ros was an expert at forging mom's signature, so getting my "F" papers signed was a breeze.

My attitude about school was that passing is passing; whether with an A or a D, it was all the same. I turned my homework in when I felt like it, seldom studied, and during class, I was very distracted. As much as I hated school, I never wanted to fail or get held back though. Some days, I would be a class clown for attention; other times, I would be disrespectful to teachers just to pass the time. I daydreamed out the window often. Regardless of what I was doing, I was miserable. I hated school... I hated my life... I allowed a group of girls to convince me that everyone hated me and wanted me dead.

The truth of the matter was that everyone did not hate me. Those who picked on me were just kids who had issues within themselves and chose me as an easy target.

CHAPTER THREE

RUN NO MORE

I was invited to a slumber party, so I asked my mom if I could attend. She said yes. The girl who was throwing the party was known for having the best parties in the school. I was excited that I was included. In order to ride someone else's bus after school, you needed a signed note from your parents. My mom signed the note so that Friday after school, I was able to ride bus 10 to go to the party. Everyone was talking about how much fun we were going to have. After class, I grabbed my bag of clothes and proceeded to bus 10. Right before I got on the bus, a random person approached me.

"Do you know why you got invited to the slumber party?" he asked me.

I turned, looked at the boy and then shook my head.

"Those girls had you invited in order to jump you," he said.

"Oh," was what could come out of my mouth.

I was devastated. By this time, my bus had already left, so I turned around and went back inside the school to call my mom for her to pick me up. My weekend was tough because I couldn't comprehend why people wanted to hurt me. Why would someone go through that much trouble for little ol' me? How could they be so evil and mean? Monday rolled around, and it was school as normal. A friend of mine who was also invited but couldn't attend confirmed that the party was in fact a setup.

I was upset yet thankful for the news of a random

stranger. Somehow, some way, God always watched over me and kept me safe because "No weapon formed against me shall prosper..." — Isaiah 54, Holy Bible.

I never thought the day would come when I stopped running, but after a while, I got tired of being afraid and feeling like a coward. After class, I was going to confront Cheryl once and for all. Enough was enough! The bell rang, and I went straight up to her and said,

"If you wanna' fight, let's fight!"

I wasn't afraid of fighting one-on-one but was terrified of being killed while being jumped. I watched several gang movies on the weekend and saw how people were stomped to death. I was fearful that it would happen to me. The other side of the track was infested with drugs and crime, so most of the kids who lived there were used to getting into trouble. Many of their fathers were not active in their lives, and some of their mothers were addicted to drugs. After more than a year of running and strategizing, I couldn't allow myself to run anymore. The bully who made my life a living hell always had so much to say when she was with her crew but never said anything to me when we were in class.

I went straight up to her when she was alone and said,

"You always talkin shit with your girls... you wanna' fight!!! Let's do this!" I guess I caught her off guard because everyone was so used to me cowering down. I was to the point where I didn't care if I got beat up as long as they knew that I wasn't running from them anymore. She talked smack, and for the first time, I talked smack right back. When she yelled at me, I yelled back. When she barked, I barked back! I was ready to fight! Because of the scene we were making in the hall, we both were escorted to the office by a teacher. The teacher had us go to separate rooms. While I waited in the room assigned to me, I heard her in the office next to mine crying. I couldn't believe it. She seemed so tough. Why would she be in the office crying? I overheard her say that I started the whole thing. They kept us in the office until the buses were scheduled to pull off. They radioed to our buses and had them stay behind so we had a way home.

The next day, I arrived at school with Vaseline smeared on my face. I was wearing my oversized green winter coat, which extended past my knees. In my coat pockets I had my keychain, which had several keys and a mini police baton. I also had a Knee-high and a thick pink sock both filled with C batteries. This time, I was looking for Cheryl. They taught me what fighting gear was all about. I had enough! I was ready to fight, but I couldn't find her. The sweet, timid girl became enraged. The anger grew stronger and caused me to misbehave in school more than usual. My behavior landed me in a couple of detentions with the kids I once feared. Being in detention with them wasn't as scary after all. Once they heard about me standing up to Cheryl, most of them stopped bullying me. A few days passed with no drama or issues, so I thought things died down with Cheryl, but I was mistaken. She and her friends found a ride to my neighborhood, knocked on my door and told me to come out to fight. There were at least twenty girls outside of my apartment shouting my name. I'm so glad my dad was home because he stopped my mom from going out to fight just like my sister did in Palm Lakes. My mom shouted out the window, "18 and older, I'm gonna' kick your ass!!"

My family never allowed anyone to hurt me. My dad calmed my mom down then shouted out the window that he was going to call the cops. The crowd dispersed.

The next day, my mom went up to the school again and expressed her deep concern, but once again, the school showed no regard for what my mother was sharing since no one had actually hurt me (yet).

The following day, a student went to the main office and made them aware that I was walking through the halls swinging around my sock with batteries in it. I heard that I was reported, so I put the sock in my locker. The school searched my locker and found my sock sitting on the top shelf. I was suspended from school for two weeks. The school called my parents, who had left their jobs early, to pick me up. I sat in the back seat of their van with my head down. My mom turned from the passenger seat, lifted my head, looked me square in the eyes and said,

"You're not bad; you're just hurt."

"You're not in trouble for getting suspended. I know you were just trying to protect yourself." "I'm going to send you to a school where you'll be safe and won't have to worry anymore," my dad decreed.

My parents understood and loved me when I didn't know how to love myself.

Once I turned fifteen, much older men started to show interest in dating me. I was young, but still knew that something was wrong with men almost the age of my father asking to take me out. As a matter of fact, there was an older man in my neighborhood who I hung out with for several months. He was always a perfect gentleman. To me, he was like an older brother, very laid back and easy to talk to. When I hung out with him,

I felt like an adult, free to do whatever I wanted, which wasn't much, but just the thought was good enough for me. In his living room, he had a black leather couch and a loveseat.

Behind his couch was a large, framed image of a black cougar standing in front of a gold pyramid. He had black venetian blinds in his windows and a shelf with tons of different fragranced air fresheners and incense. I liked having a place to hang out without feeling like I was under the direction of grownups.

When it was time for him to pay me for light dusting and washing a few dishes, which didn't feel like work at all, I looked at him and beamed.

"I don't want money," I told him without mincing my words.

He looked up into my eyes and smiled. I could tell that he was surprised and baffled at my sudden outburst. He had merely raised a brow.

"If you don't want money, what do you want?" He was staring into my eyes, wondering what a fifteen-year-old would want apart from money.

"I want a pair of Tims," I told him.

The man had smiled and then burst into a row of laughter.

"Your wish is my command, my lady…" He grinned. He drove me to the mall, and I sat back in the passenger seat, already picturing myself in a fresh pair of Tims. I was so excited I didn't care to hide it. Once we reached the mall, he parked his car and we both walked in.

"You can pick out any pair of Tims you want," he had informed me and at that moment, I felt like the world was in my pocket.

I searched for the camel color, waterproof Nubuck

Leather upper boots just like the boys on the block wore. I planned to allow the tongue of the boots to flap forward while the loose laces caused them to flop off my feet with each step I took. I couldn't find what I wanted, and he seemed to notice my disappointment.

"What's up lady?" he asked me, searching my face.

"I can't find what I want," I sadly told him.

"Is that so?" he asked, and I nodded at him.

"Since you can't find what you really want, how bout' I drive you back home and then we come back in a couple of weeks? I'm sure new stocks will be in, and you can choose what you want." I simply shook my head. I didn't want this opportunity to pass me by. Eager to leave the store with something, I settled for a pair of camel-colored Timberland Euro Hiker Boots. They were cool, but not as cool as my initial choice. I tried them on and walked to the register in order for the cashier to scan the box. I wanted to preserve the newness, so I placed them back in the box and proceeded to his car. I was hype to finally have a pair of Tims!

As we drove home, I rummaged through the bag, eager to get home and wear them around the house. My parents weren't alarmed when I came home with new clothes because they knew I earned money babysitting my neighbor and I always had funds from watching my cousin during the summer. He pulled around the corner of my house to let me out. I was ecstatic, so I gave him a hug and thanked him. He asked me for a kiss, so I gave him a kiss on the cheek. No harm in an innocent kiss on his cheek; he was my older brother who just bought me a new pair of Tims! He grabbed my face and attempted to slide his tongue in my mouth. I was disgusted. I thought I was his little sister! I slammed the door to his BMW and ran home. I was extremely upset about him attempting to kiss me inappropriately. I trusted him. How could he betray my trust? I was just a kid compared to him... I never told my parents because I didn't want him to go to jail. I just put this incident, along with many others, in my little box and buried it far, far away in my mind.

A few weeks passed, and I heard his boomin' system as he drove through the neighborhood. I knew it was him because he always blasted True Playa by Biggie any time he got to my block. He pulled up beside me and asked if I wanted to get McDonald's; he knew how much I loved Big Macs with extra cheese and a hot fudge sundae with extra fudge and nuts. It was fun sneaking out of the neighborhood in someone else's car while blaring H-Town to maximum capacity. He even allowed me to drive the Beemer from time to time. Looking at him sitting behind the steering, I remembered how he tried to stick his tongue into my mouth a couple of weeks ago.

I was filled with disgust, wanting to scream at him, but I held back. I reminded myself to stay calm, and thankfully, I succeeded.

"Get in the car," he tried to cajole again.

"You ain't my friend no more," I sneered at him.

He had looked up at me as if I had slapped him. "Why not?"

"Just leave me alone!" I shouted.

He sped off. I never saw him after that day.

CHAPTER FOUR

Lean Against the Brick

My parents always taught me to say no to drugs. I completed Drug Abuse Resistance Education programs, which my school offered each year, beginning at kindergarten. Although the education was valuable, it wasn't what stopped me from trying drugs. What stopped me from trying drugs was witnessing the behavior of my neighbor, who was addicted to crack. I would watch her six-year-old daughter in order for her to do her drugs. It was my responsibility to keep her daughter safe while she got high; it was easy money for me, so I didn't mind much. I was happy that I was able to keep her daughter safe. I watched her daughter in her bedroom while she did her drugs in the living room, but I preferred to take her to the park or for ice cream. I had to keep her daughter occupied and safe for a minimum of three hours. Outside of her drug addiction, I think my neighbor was a pretty good parent. Most drug addicts didn't even think about their children, but my neighbor did. She loved her daughter very much, but sometimes, she got depressed and had to escape her reality by turning to drugs.

I was in the living room waiting to leave to pick up her daughter from the bus stop. I forgot my bag, so I opened her bedroom door, not knowing she was in there. I witnessed her taking off her clothes in front of a man who was known as a dirty drug addict. I was shocked to see her preparing to have sex with someone who barely changed his clothes. I stood at the door disturbed. She looked back at me and made eye contact; I immediately slammed the door and left to pick her daughter up from the bus stop as planned. While I was walking to the bus stop I was very upset. Why would she have sex with Jerome? She was the same age as my mother, so I couldn't tell her what to do. I wanted her to be okay and to make good decisions. Everyone knew Jerome was a heavy drug addict who wore the same clothes for weeks on end. He would speed-walk up and down the streets, looking for drugs. Everyone knew him. He never bothered us. He would only walk up and down the street asking us if we knew where he could find some crack.

When my neighbor wasn't high, she was tons of fun to hang out with, and even though she was a drug addict, she was still a good person. The thing was, she was dealt a few tough cards in life. She was injured while in the military, which caused her honorable discharge. The weight of her injury became so unbearable it led her to drug use. She and I started to hang out more; she said we were like sisters. I liked having another big sister and having a place to hang out without any strict parental instructions.

I was bored sitting in my parents' house, so I decided to go hang out with her. She invited me in and told me she was about to do her drugs because her daughter was with her grandmother for the weekend.

"Care for some?" she asked me with a daring look.

I looked at the stuff in her hands, and I knew I never wanted to have anything to do with drugs. "Nah, I'm good," I told her in a firm voice. I didn't want her to ever doubt the fact that I didn't want to ever do drugs, and I didn't want her to offer that stuff to me again. After I had declined her offer, I quickly went into her bedroom and lay on the bed to watch TV. She knew I hated the fact that she did drugs; why would she bother to ask me to do it with her? When she was finished doing her drugs, she playfully yelled for me to come out. She had a small sandwich bag with a crack rock inside, and she was holding a small thin tube. She then told me that she wanted to show me how she does her drugs even if I didn't want to try it. I responded by saying,

"I don't ever want to know what to do with it if someone were to give it to me."

In her kitchen drawer were a few burnt spoons with crooked handles. Occasionally, I would see white powder on the kitchen table and counters, which I ignored.

A couple of the neighborhood kids tried crack and told me it was the best high anyone could ever have. I told them that I feared turning into a crackhead one day, so I had no interest in trying it even once. It only takes one shot before I could get addicted or die and I wasn't open to taking that risk! They provided me with examples of a few older people in our neighborhood who seemed to have it together yet did crack on occasions. We referred to them as ol' heads. They were older than us by about seven years, had their own place, were working, but they were still hip and sometimes gave us alcohol and allowed us to party with them. The neighborhood kids tried hard to convince me that doing crack is okay every once in a while, as long as I had a strong mind. They said that if I had a strong mind, then I would never get addicted. I absolutely had a strong mind. I was strong enough to resist peer pressure when something offered would alter my mind or body to an uncontrollable level or even kill me. I had no interest in discovering what it felt like to get high on crack. All I kept in the back of my mind was if I ever did drugs, I would lose control of my senses and begin to have sex with other drug addicts who don't bathe or change their clothes.

I was scared I would sell my body for crack and lose myself completely. I was scared straight! I never tried hard drugs and never will!

"I shall not die, but live, and declare the works of the Lord"—Psalm 118:17, KJV.

I had a nice-sized click of girls who had my back and didn't mind fighting to protect me. In my neighborhood I was known as a fighter so any chance I had to fight, I took it. It was a great way to get out some of the anger I harbored. I was no longer alone and always had people to stand with me during difficult times.

The girls from the other side of the track wanted to fight us specifically because of where we lived. There were just as many of us as there were them. They called us out, so we were going to go throw down. On our way to fight the girls from the other side of the track, we received word that they all had knives, so we turned around and went into our homes to grab knives, too. I opened the drawer and grabbed the largest kitchen knife that I could find. I told my mom that I loved her and would be home soon. She had no idea what I was planning to do. She didn't know how caught up I was. While walking out the door, I showed my older sister the large knife and told her what was about to happen. Ros tried everything within her power to make me stay home, but I wouldn't listen. I grabbed the knife and ran out the house. I looked up at my sister from the parking lot as she looked down from our apartment window; I said bye because I thought I was going to die that day. I didn't want to hurt anyone, but they called me out, so I felt like I had to defend myself. I got in the car with my girls and proceeded to drive to meet the group of girls who also had weapons.

As I replayed the story, I realized how foolish my actions were. I was going to fight girls with knives and thought that if I pulled my knife out, it would have kept them away. I didn't want to stab anyone. I just wanted to protect myself. I was only a kid fighting to survive.

I can't thank my sister enough for calling the police that day. When we were halfway to the other side of the track, the police were trailing us, so we quickly pulled over and threw our knives out the car window. We went home to live another day.

How often do we see children on the news who shot or killed people at their school? They may not have had any plans of hurting anyone but only wanted to make a bully stop picking on them... What if carrying a weapon was the only way they knew out of their situation? A lot of people sit back, condemning others without a clue about what people go through, especially children.

Take the time to care! Take the time to listen! Be kind, even when people don't deserve it because you never know how hard it is for some people to just get out of their bed.

I brought a knife because I was tired of getting beaten up and only wanted to protect myself. I thought that if they witnessed me holding a knife, it would have made them leave me alone.

What would have happened if we had all ended up killing each other, or if we went to a juvenile detention center or jail?

If I had died that day, would I have been known as a troubled kid who had intentions of harming others?

Would I have been known as a terrorist? Or would I have been known as a kid who was hurting inside and knew no other way out?

Never in a million years did I think I would make it this far, but someone needed to hear my story! We endure specific challenges to help someone else along the way. I faced many challenges to ensure that others wouldn't repeat the same mistakes I made. If I had let the fear of being judged stop me from publishing this book, those who are meant to learn from my story might remain as troubled as I once was. Additionally, those who feel unworthy might continue to believe that lie. I will not let that happen. I will not allow my battle scars to be in vain.

I share my story because you can't see the struggles I've faced just by looking at me. Some readers might judge me based on my actions as a child, while others may learn from my experiences.

Which one will you be?

There was never a dull moment in my neighborhood. Kiara was a spoiled kid who lived with her grandparents. They lived about six minutes' walk from my house. She attended a special school for troubled kids. She and I hung out when my main crew wasn't around. Because she was a bit challenging for her grandparents, they bribed her with rewards, treats, money and prizes in order to get her to behave. Sometimes, they would buy her a 40-ounce of malt liquor if she promised to stay in the house and be good. Her grandparents seemed to truly care about her; they were good people, and they did the best they could. Kiara's room was filled with everything a child could possibly want. There was a radio, a large color TV, a daybed, a closet full of the latest fashions, plenty of shoes, and a wall covered in posters. Whatever a kid desired, she had it all. She was one of the first kids on the block to get the new Xcape and SWV CDs and the only kid I knew with their own room. We would sing the entire Xcape Album all hours of the night pretending we were stars. We talked about one day starting our own singing group and being just like them. She was the only one who could hold a note, so I agreed to sing in the background. We began the night by singing "Weak" by SWV and ended with "Just Kick It" by Xscape.

It was about 7:00 PM and it was time to make my way home. This evening, I sensed that something was wrong. You know that gut feeling, that knot in your stomach? Well, that's what I felt. I usually walked home alone, but I felt uneasy and didn't understand why. Something just didn't seem right, but I couldn't put my finger on it. I told Kiara that something was telling me to go the long way home and not to cut through the apartments as I usually did. After going back and forth with her she convinced me that everything would be fine. She offered to walk me home and assured me that nothing would happen to me. I was cool with her walking with me but insisted we take the long way this time. She won me over with her persistence. I agreed to cut through the apartments like always. I wasn't alone; she said she had my back.

As we were taking the shortcut to my house, she continued to reassure me that no one was in our hood who wanted to do me harm and if someone did, in fact, roll up, it would be me and her against them. I insisted that something bad was about to happen as we crossed through the first court. No one was in sight. I guess she was right. I must have been overreacting like she said. I

had one more court to go, and then I would be just about
home. Right before I was going to cut through the final
court to get home, a group of five grown women rolled
up in a car. I was about sixteen years old and everyone
in the car were adults out of high school. Cheryl's
cousin exited the car while holding her 40-ounce bottle
of Red Bull, the others followed. "You got beef with my
cousin?" she asked me, eyeing me from head to toe. She
was wearing tight blue jeans and a plain white T-Shirt
for men. Before I could respond, I saw punches coming
from every direction. As I was getting jumped by grown
women because of some kid stuff at school, I could only
think of survival. Because I was a quick thinker, I decided
to lean against the brick wall next to the Laundromat
door. I took as many punches as I could while swinging
back as hard and as fast as I could. I knew that if I hit
the ground, they would stomp the hell out of me, and
I would probably die. I hated my life but I didn't want
to go out like that. I thought to myself, just keep
swinging, and eventually, it would be all over. So that
was exactly what I did. I tried to dodge as much as I
could. I was getting tired; the pain was intense, but I
just kept swinging while mentally coaching myself to
keep a tight stance and not to fall. I was petrified! These
chicks rolled up on me out of the blue and just started
pounding on me. I looked over at Kiara who said that
she had my back. She too was petrified. She stood there
frozen. I looked at her while mentally crying for help!
She continued to watch in fear.

I threw punches and took punches. I was no match
for five girls. They were wearing me out. After a while,
one of the boys on the block jumped in and pulled the
girls off me. When the beating was over, the five girls

got in their car and left. I was left beaten physically, mentally and emotionally. I zipped up my black and white Adidas jacket that they were trying to take while beating me up and managed to hold my tears in until I got home. I only had a court to go. I was confused as to why grown women would want to beat on a sixteen-year-old kid. My mother, older cousins or any adult I knew would never beat up a kid and be proud of it. How could they feel good about what they just did? They knew I was a kid, and on top of that, I was so much smaller than them. I looked at Kiara and said

"At least I didn't fall."

In my mind I felt like I won since I didn't run, I fought back, and I didn't fall, but deep down, it made me feel even more worthless. Kiara walked me home, came upstairs in my room and hugged me. She cried with me!

I pushed her away and said, "Why didn't you have my back?"

She continued to apologize, but it wasn't enough for me. I trusted her, and she didn't step up like she said she would. I would have gone down fighting with her if the tables were turned. She came over a few times after that, but things weren't the same. Eventually we just stopped hanging out. I had no desire to continue our friendship.

I figured if I continued to fight a lot, eventually, I would get so good that people would leave me the heck alone. On the outside, I appeared tougher, but I was dying inside.

My wardrobe included many items a guy would wear, such as oversized baggy jeans, lumberjack shirts, cartoon character tees, and items from brands like Cross

Colours, Karl Kani, Tommy Hilfiger, Dickies, Carhartt, and Timberland. For kicks, I wore Nike, Fila and my one pair of Tims. I wore large gold bamboo earrings and tied my ponytail so tightly that it made my eyes appear chinky. Jam hair gel allowed me to slick my edges nice and tight. I wrapped my ponytail with a bandana or spread it out like peacock feathers sticking straight up from the center of my head. No matter how confident I appeared on the outside, I just couldn't understand why people were against me or why I always had to fight.

The night I gave up my purity was one of the worst nights of my life. I was the only girl in my crew that was untouched and was constantly teased because of it. Sara was a super cool girl from Texas. She and I hung out a lot after school and on the weekends. She lived with her mother and little sister close to the other side of the track. Her father and mother divorced, so she moved to Jersey. She spoke highly of her dad and visited him on holidays. Anytime I wanted to hang out, it was never a problem. Sara didn't even have to ask. I would just show up, and she would say,

"Mom, is it okay if Wendy spends the night?"

Her mom always said yes. The night I gave my innocence was preplanned with a "man" I didn't love. I told my mom I was going to spend the night at Sara's house and instead spent the night with him. His house wasn't clean. He didn't do anything special for me, and he sure didn't love me. We were dating for a while, and sex was expected. While in his cousin's house sitting on her bed. I told him that I didn't want to have sex with him.

"I don't wanna' have sex with you," I told him, already having cold feet.

He smiled at me and then said, "Why not?"

I looked at him from head to toe and wondered what I was doing with him in the first place. I suddenly wanted to go back home to my mom.

"I want to call my mom," I nervously told him in a hush tone.

I shared what she always told me, which was "no matter what I ever do wrong or if I get in a jam, I should call her, and she will come get me no matter what time of night it was." She always told me that "no matter what I did; she would never stop loving me."

Her voice came to mind as I sat on his cousin's unmade bed, feeling uncomfortable. A part of me wanted to have sex because I heard the girls in school talk about how they were now women because of it, but a bigger part just wanted to go home to my family. It was about 3:00 AM and I was still contemplating for hours about having sex. "I will just call my mom and tell her what I did," I told him, feeling bad for myself.

"What! Are you crazy? Won't your mom be mad at you?" he asked in disbelief. But I didn't care; I just wanted to go home.

"I know I'll get into trouble..." I began, feeling like a child who had suddenly became rebellious, but then I continued in a small voice I didn't recognize as my own, "...But I also know that she will come pick me up and help me work through this."

"I don't have a phone," he simply told me, spreading his hands.

It was way too late to call Sara or walk back to her house, so I was stuck spending the night with him either way. When it was over, I felt hurt.

That's it!

I thought to myself, feeling regretful, guilty and

shameful.

That's what all the girls in school been talking about? It was nothing like how the girls described it; it was horrible. The next day, he dropped me off at Sara's and I went home as if nothing ever happened. It didn't bring us closer. It didn't make us fall in love. I gave one of my most valuable possessions away to a man who didn't even appreciate it.

To my young queens and kings reading this, I strongly advise you to WAIT! You're not missing out on anything… Save yourself for your husband or wife! Premarital sex is overrated. There are a lot of risks involved when giving your body to someone! Think twice!

I enjoyed spending time with my family in PA, especially my cousin Andrew. Back then, we called him Drew Lue. Hyde Gal was their friendly and loving red Irish Setter. Aunt Terry called her Drew's sister. Drew and I were inseparable since birth. He has always accepted and loved me for me. Even to this day, I refer to him as a cousin- brother versus first cousin because he and I are just that close. We are closer than most siblings.

During the summer I babysat Antonio, my other cousin, while Drew worked at Burger King. At the end of the summer we would go school shopping with all the money we saved from our summer jobs. The first day of school was a real-deal fashion show. The night before our first day, we would lay out all our clothes on the couch; our new shoes and socks were on the floor directly in front of the couch. Besides our shoes were our book bags and school supplies. I was constantly in trouble back home, so my mom and dad decided to have me try a school in West Chester. My aunt, my mom's identical twin, and my uncle agreed to take care of me for the school year. Then, based on my behavior, they would decide whether to allow me to stay. For the first time in my life, I kind of, sorta liked school because my cousin was with me, I wasn't being bullied, and my aunt was very active in my studies. I stopped lying about not having homework and sat down at the dining room table with her each day to study. She had a fancy job in Corporate America, and after a long, stressful day at work, she always made time for me.

It meant a lot to know that she wanted me to do well in school. I looked forward to making her proud.

My grades started to improve, and my self-esteem started to increase slightly. Until one day, I did something stupid and was sent back home the first month of school. I was bored while walking to my class, so I pulled the fire alarm and ran. I was easily bored and did foolish things for my own personal entertainment. I saw it in a movie and was curious as to what it would be like to pull it. We were told that if the alarm panel was pulled it would squirt ink. I wondered if it was true and had to see for myself. Nothing squirted out. Thank goodness there were no cameras. I never got caught! If that wasn't enough, I sprayed mace in one of the hallways the following period. Someone saw me and told on me. I was suspended, so my aunt and uncle sent me back home to "bully-town." They were diligent regarding my education and ensured that I knew I was loved and protected. I was just a bored kid who did many foolish things. My aunt and uncle were stricter than my parents and had zero tolerance for misbehaving, especially with me being a girl. They just wanted me to be their little princess, the daughter they never had, but I was a troubled kid who didn't know how to process my hurt and anger.

The fondest memory that I share with my cousin brother is sneaking out at night to get Dairy Queen. When my aunt and uncle went to bed, Drew and I snuck out the back door. He would quickly ride his silver BMX to Dairy Queen to pick up a chocolate Oreo blizzard for me and a cookie dough blizzard for himself. We would sneak back into the house and enjoy ice cream in his room. After we ate our ice cream, we snuck back outside to take a dip in the Community Center pool by pushing our way through a small hole at the bottom of the high chain link fence. The pool was about five steps from his house, so we had to be careful not to wake my aunt and uncle by splashing too loud. I stayed close to Drew because I couldn't swim.

He is eleven months and twenty-seven days younger than me, but I always looked to him as an older brother.

When we hung out, I was considered the bad kid and he was the angel until I started to rub off on him. Because we shared the same fence with the neighborhood pool, during summer mornings, we would throw things out of Drew's bedroom window at the people swimming. Before they looked up to see where the items were coming from, we ducked. I became a little too courageous and threw one of his sneakers out the window. Unfortunately, it hit one of the lifeguards, who was my aunt's former teacher, in the head. The lifeguard came to the house with the shoe and told my aunt that someone had thrown it from her house. My aunt answered the door and recognized her son's shoe. She looked at me and knew I did it. My face always told on me. As a kid, anyone could look at me and know whether I was guilty based on the strange look I plastered on my face.

My aunt punished us by making us sit on the steps.

Drew would sit at the top of the steps and I had to sit at the bottom. We hated being separated, so having us on opposite ends of the steps made us sad, but of course, we never allowed anything or anyone to separate us so when my aunt would leave the room, we would throw things at each other and run up and down the stairs, when she would come back in the room we would separate and pretend we were sitting in our assigned spots all along. I was a scaredy-cat since age four and didn't grow out of it until my late teens. At night Drew and I would watch Tales from the Crypt. I would duck my head under the covers until the introduction concluded, then would watch the remainder of the show. After watching Tales from the Crypt, I was afraid to go to sleep so I would make noises and pull on his nose all night to try to keep him up. Many nights we prank called people, ordered take out to other people's homes or stayed up all night pretending to be chefs in the kitchen. Tree Street was one of the best places of my childhood! I love that house in West Chester!

I love you, Drew Lue, The Blooptah Bleep.

CHAPTER FIVE

TQ

After transferring from Flopper High to West Chester, getting suspended from West Chester, I was back in Jersey at yet another school. At this school, I made friends quickly and easily but still carried many deep-rooted scars and tons of baggage. School work was still not at the top of my priority list. I continued to do just enough to get by, as I always did. Because of my experience with books and lockers, I didn't bother to ever carry books. I rarely remembered my locker combination since I never used it, despite not feeling threatened.

Instead of carrying a notebook, I would fold one or two sheets of paper and place them in the back pocket of my jeans. I kept my ink pen in my front pocket. The students at this school were very kind, so if I needed a book for class, someone was always willing to lend it. If I felt like taking notes, I would use the same crumpled-up piece of paper from my back pocket throughout the day. Sometimes, I would use the same papers for several weeks, depending on my mood and whether I felt like it. Once I filled the paper with notes from various classes, I would discard it. I never kept papers for long.

In class, I often daydreamed or passed notes when teachers turned their backs. Our way of communicating was to write notes and exchange them in the hallway while going to our next class.

Even though I didn't care much for school, my favorite subject was science. I was fascinated by protons, neutrons, and electrons. I loved everything about science.

I never realized how much I enjoyed science, especially in Flopper because I was so distracted with survival. I actually paid attention during science class at my new school and on a good day I would take notes on both sheets of paper.

Physical Education was the only class in which I received an A+. It was easy; all I had to do was dress out and participate. I enjoyed PE, so I was highly engaged and active. I even made the all-star basketball team. I was pretty good at basketball when I focused, but when I became overly excited, I fouled the heck out of people. I loved this school the most because that's where I met my husband. I'm grateful for everything I experienced because if I hadn't gone through those challenges, I wouldn't have been transferred and wouldn't have met the love of my life. It's funny how so much good can come from so much bad.

I was getting settled into my new school and had made plenty of friends. The girls were talking about the new boy, but no one had seen him yet. My friends and I speculated about what he looked like and where he might be from down south. When he walked through the hall, my girls and I discussed who would snatch him up. Once I saw him, I immediately said, "he's mine." Each time a new boy came to our school, we would decide who would get him. My girls always took first dibs because I never cared much about that stuff until I saw TQ.

His complexion was so smooth and brown. It was like milk chocolate. He wore his hair in long, shiny braids and spoke with a strong southern twang! He was the coolest kid in school, even on his very first day! He seemed a little shy; I liked that too. He dressed, spoke, and behaved differently from the other boys, which made him shine even brighter in my eyes. All the girls in my crew wanted him, but I claimed him, so my girls knew they had to back up. I kept my eyes on them, though. Girls are snaky, especially in high school.

For the first time in my life, I was extremely assertive towards a boy. I went right up to TQ and introduced myself. After talking to him and trying to understand what he was saying due to his thick Southern accent, I became increasingly intrigued. Although I could barely understand what he said, I still liked him a lot. His accent was so strong that I had to listen carefully and try to form a sentence with the few keywords I could understand. Every day I saw him, my desire for him grew stronger. I was determined to make him mine. We started hanging out after school with mutual friends. TQ and I shared many similarities, such as both of our parents serving in the military, enjoying the same music, and having a similar style of clothing. He lived on McGuire, AFB, right around the corner from where I grew up. TQ stayed fresh all day every day. He coordinated a hat with each outfit, and his shoes and backpack always matched. He wore wooden African beads and snow goggles on his hat which made him look so dope! He always smelled so good. After he walked by, the scent of his cologne lingered, making me feel warm and fuzzy inside. He sagged his oversized pants, often pulling one leg up or rolling both pant legs tightly down to his ankles. He rocked his braid or "Hollow Point" bullet belt with the remainder of the leather hanging at the front of his pants.

Sometimes, he wore gold fronts and sported a huge hoop silver nose ring or a Tupac diamond. No matter what he wore, he was always the coolest dude on the block!

Beyond his charm, he was considerate, polite, and genuinely cared about my feelings. For the first time in my life, outside of my father, I met a true gentleman.

After a few months of hanging out, I called him and told him that I wanted to be his girlfriend. Guess there's a first time for everything. I never asked a boy out before, nor have I actively pursued anyone. However, I finally met someone I truly wanted that I didn't care about pursuing. I had never even tried to be with a boy, but I wanted TQ and I was going to get him.

After I called him and told him that I wanted to be his girlfriend, I briefly wondered what would happen to my pride if he rejected me. However, I quickly dismissed those thoughts because TQ and I seemed to get along well, and our friendship had been thriving.

"Can I be your girlfriend?" I asked him, trying to sound confident despite my nerves.

"Yes," he said. I heard him smiling through the phone. I blinked, trying to process what he had just told me. He said yes!! I was his girl!

I felt like I hit the jackpot when he agreed to be my boyfriend. The foundation of our friendship made our relationship much stronger. We enjoyed listening to Scarface, Wu-Tang, Ghostface, Method Man, Mobb Deep, A Tribe Called Quest, Heltah Skeltah and KRS-One. TQ also created his own raps while selling mixtapes. He used a notebook to record his artworks and creative lyrics.

After we became serious, it was time for him to meet my parents. He caught a cab from McGuire to my house which was a little over thirty minutes away. He arrived wearing baggy brown jeans with one pant leg pushed up, an oversized long-sleeved brown baseball shirt featuring cartoon characters on the front, two-toned tan K-Swiss boots, and a black 76ers trench coat. His mouth was filled with gold teeth. Let's not forget his huge silver hoop nose ring, which you could see a mile away. It was about the size of a nickel. He wore a brown baseball cap turned to the side, matching the color of his shoes perfectly. His long, well-manicured braids peeked out from under the brim of the hat and reached his shoulders.

I looked out the window and saw the Rainbow Cab logo on the car, and I became more ecstatic! I ran down the steps of my apartment to greet my man, who leaned against his wooden African cane. My mom looked out the window and chuckled. Playfully, she said to my dad, "Look what Mee brought home." When I was a baby, my family affectionately called me Nee Nee. As I got older, my parents began calling me Mee Mee, and sometimes just Mee for short. My mom changed the name because she said I reminded her of herself, and I take pride in that. My dad also gave me a special nickname, Meemers, which I still love to be called to this day. There are many variations of my name!

My parents didn't care about his ethnicity, income level, or appearance. What mattered to them was that I found someone who made me feel good about myself, kept me out of trouble, and motivated me to aspire to greater things. Besides God, TQ was the best thing that ever happened to me at that time of my life. He was the first boy I brought home and the only boy welcomed in my parent's house! My parents were overjoyed to finally meet the person who brought me so much happiness. When I misbehaved and was placed on punishment, I was unable to have company or go outside, but he was still allowed to come over. My mom said that once he came into my life, I became renewed. She wasn't going to do anything to make me revert to the depressed teenager who spent many weekends alone watching the show Cops all day.

TQ helped shift my focus to achieving good grades in school through his consistent encouragement and support.

I started to put in more effort at school and quickly improved from a "D-" student to earning all "B's" and "C's." Despite having TQ as my great motivator, I never fully committed to my studies. I completed a full year at my new school with good grades. I became respectful towards the teachers and stopped receiving detentions. School was cool, but I still lived in the same apartment complex where the girls from the other side of the track would occasionally ride through, hoping to catch me alone. Some days, they would see me outside with several of my girls and simply drive on by.

I knew to never roll through their hood alone, and the same applied to mine. There was a place in between where we both lived, which we referred to as the "Neutral Zone." Both sides were supposed to be able to come and go freely. I was standing at the payphone about to put a quarter in to call TQ since my mom hid the phones because I was in trouble again. Some ol' heads rolled up on me, threw a large cup of water on me, then pulled off. The girls from the other side of the track have many sisters and cousins who were much older and didn't hesitate to pick on younger kids. That day they either didn't feel like fighting or they actually respected the code of the "Neutral Zone."

School was out for the summer, and it was time to celebrate my transition to a better school that offered greater opportunities. For the first time, I felt peace and had a wonderful boyfriend who treated me with love and respect. I no longer spent my days alone in my room watching the show "Cops." Instead, I began going out and making new friends, forming my own click. My click and I hung out the entire summer. We got dressed up just to stand around, get pizza from the corner store or hang out with the neighborhood boys drinking 40's. When I wasn't with my friends, I was hanging out with TQ; he would either come to my house, or I would go to his.

I passed tenth grade with B's and C's at the "safe school." This environment allowed me to focus more on my studies rather than simply surviving. While I didn't fully concentrate on my education, achieving B's and C's felt remarkable to me. My mom pulled some strings to get me into this school for a year, but as summer was coming to an end, it was time to prepare for eleventh grade.

My mom shared how impressed she was by TQ because he consistently paid for a cab just to come over and sit on her couch. He always had cab fare and anything else I needed because he worked as a cook at KFC in Wrightstown, New Jersey. It was a bit unusual when TQ came over. We would all gather in the living room, watching whatever my dad had on TV. TQ and I would sit on the couch, while my dad occupied his comfy chair, doing his crossword puzzles next to us, and my mom sat in the chair directly across from him. After several months of TQ visiting and proving he was a good guy, my parents finally started going into their room during his visits, allowing us some time alone in the living room. I cherished our private time together, whether we were cuddling on the couch or stealing kisses when no one was watching. Every weekend, he would come over, and we would watch "Roots" until around 10:00

PM. After that, he would call a cab to go home. Once he got home, he would call me, and we would spend the entire night talking, often until the next morning. Sometimes, we would even fall asleep on the phone. The few times when we actually hung up from our phone conversation, we would go back and forth.

"You hang up."

"No, you hang up."

"No, you hang up first."

We would even say, "On three, we both hang up." Then we would both count to three, and neither one of us would hang up. Whenever I misbehaved, my mom would take away my phone. However, TQ would secretly lend me his brother's red Mustang phone. He would call me around the same time each night after getting home from KFC. I would hold the phone, trying to catch it before the first ring completed, so I wouldn't wake my mom from her sleep.

TQ received positive performance reviews while working at KFC and encouraged me to apply for a job there as well. Initially, I wanted to work alongside him, but they weren't hiring at the time. Instead, I decided to apply for a position at Wendy's, which was also located in Wrightstown, just up the hill from KFC where he worked.

I was sixteen when I applied for my first job. Nervous about the interview process, I asked my dad to walk me into the building. We went straight to the front counter, and I quietly stood beside him. The manager peeked out from behind the counter and instructed me to take a seat in the lobby and wait for him. My mind was flooded with thoughts.

"What should I say? What will he ask me? What if he doesn't like me?" I thought to myself, feeling a wave of nerves wash over me. The manager, Rick, approached and began asking me a few questions. I tried my best to answer them while suppressing my anxiety. "When would you be able to start work, Miss?" he asked casually.

I had no idea when I was able to start. Wrightstown was a ways from my house. I never caught a bus alone and my parents' work schedule was busy. I remembered that TQ had offered to help me get to work and would cover my cab fares until I started earning my own money. "I can start whenever you need me to," I said to Rick, my voice barely above a whisper. "How about you start this weekend?" he suggested, looking directly into my eyes. I thought to myself, "He wants me to start this weekend?" Feeling both thrilled and astonished, I realized I had never expected him to ask me to begin so soon.

"You want me to start this weekend?" I found myself asking him without even thinking.

"Yes, I want you to start this weekend. Can you do that?" he asked me in a gentle tone.

"Oh yes, I can start this weekend," I said, flashing him a smile.

"In that case, I will be expecting you," Rick had told me and then walked away. I couldn't believe it! I couldn't wait to tell TQ the good news.

True to my word, by the weekend, I was working at Wendy's. My starting salary was $5.05 an hour. I was hype! I was going to be rich!

My dad drove me back and forth to work from time to time and when he couldn't, TQ covered my cab fare until I started bringing home a check.

We took the bus to explore random places. Our first stop was 7-Eleven, where we would pick up a bus schedule. After that, we searched through the locations listed on the schedule and calculated our money to make sure we had enough fare to get to our destination and back home. Once we had our plan in place, we would hop on the bus and go sightseeing. Everything was exhilarating when we were together. Hanging with TQ was a refreshing change from my neighborhood. The guys from around my way would hit their girlfriends and even on me from time to time. I witnessed it so much that it became normal.

After I began earning a steady income, I started showering TQ with gifts. I bought him gold chains, rings, and several hoodies from a store in Browns Mills. He reciprocated by buying me gifts as well. We would often go to the mall just to treat each other. It felt wonderful to be able to buy him nice things, especially since he had always been so generous with me before I started working.

I told a couple of the girls in my click that I didn't feel like going back to Flopper. I shared that I was tired of always fighting and only desired peace. My crew was filled with fighters, so I wasn't concerned about them fighting with me, but I was tired. Although we created a name for ourselves, we weren't a real gang, but I wished we were. I watched documentaries about gangs in LA and fantasized about being a true gang banger. I thought that if I was in a real gang, I wouldn't have had to endure all the trouble and pain that I suffered as a teen. I was under the impression that gang families were better than blood families, but I now realize that no one can possibly love me more than the family I am blessed with.

I registered for school and received my schedule to return to Flopper. My girl from next door, Raven, said that she will meet me at the bus stop, and we can ride together. Then, we would meet up with the other girls from our crew. After my parents left for work, instead of going to school, I took off my school clothes, threw on some sweats, and lied on my couch to watch soaps all day. General Hospital and All My Children were my favorites. Mentally, I just didn't feel like going to school. Getting in trouble by my parents was better than fighting on my first day. I fought often and desired a break. When my parents arrived from work, they asked me how school went that day. I smiled sadly and then pouted.

"Dad, I didn't go to school today," I revealed, closely watching him.

He raised a brow and I saw him turn to look at my mom. The two exchanged a look and I knew that I had better have an explanation for them.

"Why weren't you in school, Mee?" Mom asked me. "After you guys left for work, I wasn't feeling too good, so I laid down on the couch," I explained, hoping my voice carried the weight of my words. Mom immediately sat beside me and brought her flat hand to my forehead.

"You aren't running a temp," she observed.

I nodded in agreement but wisely said nothing. "What's wrong?" my dad asked me.

"My stomach was hurting earlier, but now it doesn't hurt anymore," I lied to him. I saw them look at me with pity on their faces and I inwardly grinned.

"I guess all you need now is to lie down and rest some more," my dad said and walked into his room.

The next morning, my doorbell rang, and it was Raven. She asked me if I was going to school, and I told her no. I was in eleventh grade, and my parents trusted me to manage my own responsibilities. However, I had lost all interest in school and was planning to drop out. My parents were at a loss and didn't know what to do anymore. Cyber school didn't exist when I was in high school. They had been up to Flopper more times than I could count. They spoke to guidance counselors and tried to talk to the parents of those who were threatening me, but nothing seemed to work.

After a while, my parents became concerned about me returning to Flopper. They started to feel that we were better off exploring other alternatives. TQ suggested that I explore options for night school. He then had a conversation with my parents about the benefits of this choice, which thrilled them. I was able to complete my education without constantly looking over my shoulder. My parents felt at ease knowing that the girls who had bullied me for years would not be attending night school. This allowed me to focus on my studies again without distractions. My mom informed Flopper that I would be attending their night classes. I had made it to the eleventh grade and wanted to finish my education, so I decided to get my GED. For the first time in as long as I could remember, I truly wanted to succeed. I dedicated myself to my studies and actively participated. I gave school my all.

CHAPTER SIX

The Freedom Fight

Right outside my apartment, the guy who claimed me as his little sister got mad at me because someone told him I was talking crap about him. Instead of asking me, he approached me, yelling and saying that I "had too much mouff." After all, I had been through with the girls from the other side of the track, I refused to back down from anyone. I attempted to explain my side of the story, but he did not want to listen. He took a few steps back. I followed his lead and did the same. He put his hands up; I put mine up, too. I wasn't afraid. I figured fighting boys would only make me better equipped for anything that came my way. It would be good practice for me. After fighting so much, I started to think of it as a sport. I was always open to refining my skills of fighting. He wanted to fight me over hearsay and I was okay with it.

He was twice my size and twice my strength, but I didn't care. I wasn't running... Drama popped off quickly and easily in my hood. I was ready to take whatever he wanted to bring to me. I was also prepared to give him a little of it back. I formed a tight stance and put my hands up the way my Uncle Jimmy (RIP) showed me in his backyard in West Chester. I wasn't going to wait for him to hit me first. I knew that I had a better chance if I swung first. I swung as hard as I could while throwing my body into the punch, just like Ros taught me. It connected right in his face. Blood flew out of his mouth. I was surprised that my little fist caused so much blood, but happy at the same time. I was hoping that one blow to the face would knock him out like on TV, but it wasn't the case. Since the first blow didn't knock him down completely, I knew I was going to get it good. He touched his mouth and saw blood on his fingers, which made him even more furious. His face transformed from angry to full of rage!

He hit me so hard it felt like I was getting run over by a Mack Truck. I felt my body wanting to fall to the ground, but I wouldn't allow it to. It took all my strength to keep from falling. While standing and taking his massive punches, I started to feel sleepy, but I fought that too. My twisted way of thinking caused me to feel tough during our fight. I continued telling myself, "You're able to take massive blows from a dude and remain standing… show em' you got hands too!" I cheered myself on in my head… I had to take advantage of every opportunity to get tough in order to be prepared for future drama. There was a crowd around us watching and egging us on. I just kept swinging with all I had and so did he. He didn't take it easy on me because I'm a girl. Throughout the fight, I told myself in my mind,

"stand firm and take as much as you can." He was punching me in my face, my ribs, my arms… all over. I dodged a couple of his punches, but most of them connected. Most of my punches connected also. After what felt like hours, Raven told her boyfriend to break up the fight. "Break it up, Derek, don't let him beat Wendy up," I heard her yell at her boyfriend. When Derek pulled Tyreek off me, I got one last punch in. Before going into my house, I turned towards Tyreek, "bitch ass!" I yelled in an aggressive tone. I then spit at his feet as a sign of disrespect and proceeded towards my apartment door.

My mom was in the kitchen with her back turned to me when I walked in the door. I quickly scurried to the bathroom. Looking in the mirror, I examined my face.

The left side of my face was swollen; I had a small cut under my eye, which I figured I could easily conceal with makeup. I also had a busted lip, and my jaw was in excruciating pain. Because I was able to conceal most of the bruises and no one could see the pain that I was feeling inside, I thought I was fine. From the neck down, my entire body was black and blue. I had a sizable purple-black bruise on my left leg above my knee, about the size of a cantaloupe; the bruise wrapped around the outside of my leg into my inner thigh. I had many small cuts on the inside of my mouth and was spitting blood for the first few minutes while in the bathroom.

All I wanted to do was lie down and go to sleep, but it was way too early in the day. If I had gone to bed that early, my mom would have known that something was up. So, I shuffled around the house dodging my parents the rest of the night. I didn't tell my parents what happened because I knew if I did, they would confront the kid who was in and out of Juvie his entire life. For all I knew, the punk kids may have attempted to hurt my parents. I tried to protect them from having issues, so I kept quiet.

When everyone went to bed, I took a bag of frozen peas and placed it on my face until it completely thawed. After that, I grabbed a small box of Green Giant Broccoli & Cheese and held it against my face until it thawed as well. I went through several bags of vegetables while staying up all night, trying to reduce the swelling. I was in pain all over but refused to cry. While everyone was asleep, I was busy trying to play doctor on myself. I knew that this wasn't something I wanted to share with my sister, Ros or my parents. It was my burden to bear, and I was determined to carry on without alerting anyone.

By the early hours of the morning, I fell into an exhausted sleep, feeling pain all over my body.

The next day, I interacted with my parents but ensured that I angled myself in order to hide the left side of my face. The swelling went down a bit, which made it much easier to hide. Within a day or two of applying frozen veggies while everyone was in bed, the swelling went down entirely. The inside of my mouth was still busted, but no one was able to see that. Once all the bruises on my body had healed, I found myself back outside with the same group of people who did nothing to defend me during my time of need. I never spoke about what happened; those who witnessed it firsthand were well aware, and those who weren't there had heard about it. They also knew that I wouldn't back down or run from anyone. I had already done too much of that at Flopper.

During my time living in the apartments, I faced many negative experiences. It was an incredibly challenging period in my life. However, instead of holding on to hate and hurt, I chose to allow those experiences to make me a better person, which is my "why" regarding sharing my story with you. I refuse to be ashamed of my battle scars because I am now free. I Am No Longer A Prisoner.

I learned and grew from the pain of my past. A man should NEVER put his hands on a woman, not just a few times, not one time, NEVER. A woman should NEVER put her hands on a man, not just a few times, not one time, NEVER. Just because she is a woman does not give her the right to put her hands on a man, nor should a man justify putting his hands on a woman. There is help available for those who need assistance with self-control.

Don't be afraid to get the help you need!

I was fourteen when I felt the sting of a man hit me for the first time. My so-called boyfriend, Carl was twenty-one. My favorite radio station back then was Power 99 FM, which played the latest Hip-Hop and R&B along with jingles about malt liquor. I was sitting in the back of Carl's car, and my favorite malt liquor jingle came on the air; I began to sing along. He turned toward me with a backhanded motion in preparation to smack me because he thought I was singing about another dude. I explained that I was singing a song, causing him to become angrier. He felt I was talking back, and he thought he owned me since he was my first. In the passenger seat, his friend, Trev, turned the radio up and reiterated that I was in fact singing a song. Once Carl realized I was singing a malt liquor jingle and not a song to another dude, he rolled his eyes and said,

"you're lucky it was a song, or I was gon' whoop that ass!"

I quietly sat in the backseat fearful of making any sudden moves. He pulled up to my development a few doors down from my apartment. I got out without saying a word and entered my house as if nothing happened.

He had many young girlfriends who all looked similar. We were all of caramel complexion or lighter, petite, and naïve, and we were about the same age. We even all styled our hair in slicked-back ponytails positioned at the very top center of our heads. He thought I didn't know about them, but I did. He told me they were all

his cousins, yet I could tell there was more by the way
they looked at one another. I was pushed around from
time to time and constantly accused of doing things
that never crossed my mind. He raised his hand to hit
me any time he felt like it, causing me to cower down
whenever he needed a good stroke of his ego. It made
him feel powerful. It made him feel in control. He yelled
at me without reason and took his frustration out on
me often. When he calmed down from his temper, he
would say that he only gets angry because he loves me.
Then he would share stories with me about his tough
childhood while promising to never mistreat me again.
He sounded like a broken record. I wanted out. After
almost a year of dating Carl, I gained enough courage to
leave, but it wasn't an easy break. When I told him that
it was over, he replied by saying

"If you leave me, I'll kill you."

A part of me believed that he would, in fact, kill
me, while another part didn't care if he did. Anything
would be better than a man who constantly raised his
hand at me. Most of the time, he only raised his hand
and shouted, but the few times he hit me were far too
many. I would prefer anything over walking on eggshells,
afraid to sing or even speak.

The night I told him I was leaving him forever he
became very aggressive. He yelled and reminded me
that no one ever leaves him. He referenced his previous
words...

"If I tried to leave, he would kill me." I looked at
him deeply in his eyes, smiled and said, "I am not afraid
of you no more."

"You ain't leavin' me," he threatened me.

His tone was so forceful that it sounded more like

a roar or growl of a wild animal living in the jungle. I growled back.

"Being dead is better than being with you!!" I shot at him without an ounce of fear. He would have to suffer the consequences of whatever he planned to do to me, but I was no longer going to put up with his abuse. If he hit me again or attempted to kill me, I had every plan of going down with a fight! Even though my self-esteem was extremely low I still knew deep down inside that I was worth more. Somewhere in a tiny, faraway place, I knew I deserved better. It was not the first time I attempted to leave him, but it was the last time. That night, I walked away and never looked back! He tried to come around, giving me the same song and dance about being sorry and he couldn't live without me. He said he was sorry and didn't mean his abusive behavior, but I had no interest in entertaining his words.

The last words he said to me before he totally disappeared were, "fuck you then, bitch!"

I looked back and said,

"That's right, this bitch don't want your stankin' ass no more, so keep it pushin'!"

In that moment, he realized that I could no longer be controlled by him. He slowly walked away, knowing I would never return to him again, no matter what. Ten years later, while at Lumberton Walmart, I saw him with someone who resembled me in appearance. She was much younger than him. I said a silent prayer for her, hoping he changed his ways.

While walking through my apartment complex, I was approached by two guys who pulled out a gun on me. The guy standing on my left put the gun up to my head while having a conversation about raping me with the guy on my right. I knew that they were young punks who just wanted to flex because they had a new gun. If I backed down and showed fear, they would have most likely raped me. Instead of showing fear, I flexed back.

"You don't know who you fuckin' wit," I yelled at them in a fierce tone.

"You think we kiddin'?" one of the boys asked me.

I looked at them with cold ice that spoke of confidence, "And you think I'm fuckin' kiddin'? Touch me and this will be the last day you see daylight," I threatened them, never backing down.

"You ain't gonna' do shit," one of the boys replied, looking at me up and down.

"Try me...you ain't the only one with goons!! I got goons, too!" My voice became very loud and forceful. I projected an incredibly tough image just as I witnessed from the dudes on the block. Everything was about pulling someone's "punk card." If you show no fear and your bark is louder than theirs, you increase your chances of survival. The guy on my left pulled the gun from my head, tucked it away in the back of his jeans, under his oversized black hoodie and walked away. I thought about having a few of the boys on the block teach them a lesson but decided not to. When it comes to gun violence, it never stops until everyone is either dead or in jail. I was too concerned about someone I loved getting caught in the crossfire.

Once again, I went home and acted as if nothing ever happened. I tucked this incident and many others in the tiny box far away in my mind. I deeply love my parents and didn't want to get them involved in the street madness I faced. I was always too worried that someone might hurt them while trying to hurt me, so I stayed silent about most of the things that happened on the block.

Reflecting on my journey, I realize that it was nothing but God who brought me this far. I often take a moment to consider what might have happened if I had backed down in the face of those kids. They were at least a year younger than I was and had the audacity to point a gun at me. After the incident, I tried to move on.

For the first time in school as a teen, I actively participated in class. I completed all my homework and no longer wished to be a loud, disrespectful student. Night school was much easier because I didn't have to worry about changing classes or strategizing. I completed all my studies with flying colors. It was finally time to take the test for my GED. Math had always been my most challenging subject, so I decided to take advantage of the tutoring program offered by the night school. I arrived early in the evening for my scheduled GED test.

I felt confident yet still nervous. The big moment was facing me! I sat quietly, gripping my Number 2 pencil. At the top of the page was a space for my name, address and phone number. I wrote my name in the designated squares and shaded in the corresponding circles located underneath. Then, I flipped through the pages and answered each question to the best of my ability. I was only allowed to have the GED exam paper, a number 2 pencil, and two pieces of scratch paper. All our bags had to be placed in the front of the room. After about three hours, I completed my exam and submitted it. I left feeling confident that I would earn my GED because I had studied hard. I couldn't wait to be finished with school forever! As I left the room, the teacher told me it would take four to six weeks before I received my results. Life continued normally as I awaited my results.

I hung out with TQ on the weekend and the girls in

my click, here and there.

Three weeks later, my test results arrived in the mail. I anxiously opened the large white envelope, which had bold blue writing at the top. I started to think of a plan- b in case I didn't pass. Slowly, I slid the paper out of the envelope. The top of the letter read, "Congratulations!" I was thrilled to learn that I had achieved my GED, knowing I would never have to step foot in a school for the rest of my life. I jumped for joy and screamed with excitement before finishing the rest of the letter. Once the initial thrill wore off, I took my time to read the entire document.

The letter began with congratulations and continued on... In the middle of the page, it stated that I had exceeded the score required to obtain my General Education Diploma and was hereby being awarded a HIGH SCHOOL DIPLOMA! I couldn't believe it!! My goal was to achieve a GED. I studied hard for it, but I did even better—I earned a High School Diploma! My hard work truly paid off. I often wondered where I would have ended up if I had stayed in a regular school and applied myself, but I realize that my challenges have turned into triumphs, and I have no regrets. I am constantly reminded that I am stronger than I ever imagined. I can accomplish anything I set my mind to. I encourage YOU to dig deeply and find your strength.

Many things began to improve after I earned my High School Diploma, but my self-esteem still wasn't where it needed to be. TQ took great care of me throughout everything. He stood by my side and supported me in every way he could. He witnessed the pain I carried from being jumped, from having men beat me, and from not fitting in, which led me to feel worthless. He loved me even when I didn't love myself. He worked hard and saved up his money to move me out of the apartments, somewhere safe where I would be free. I saved up money, too. He then asked my father's permission to marry me, and I became engaged at the age of seventeen. TQ bought me a beautiful, delicate gold ring featuring a perfectly sized diamond in the center, with three smaller diamonds on each side. I could truly feel that someone loved me... I was engaged! My parents finally had peace because, for the first time in a very long time, I was Happy Being Me.

His presence significantly impacted my life in ways that I could have never imagined. I wanted better for myself and thought about a life past age twenty-one. My brokenness didn't hinder him from wanting to be with me. TQ always held my father in high regard. He consistently demonstrated that he wanted me for who I am by investing both time and money just to sit on my couch while my parents were on either side of us. He asked my father for his blessing to marry me and then sought permission for me to move in with him. The more respect he showed toward my father, the stronger my love for him grew.

"Mr. Gaines, would it be okay if Wendy moved in with me?" he asked one fateful day, and in that moment, I felt my heart melt. All TQ wanted was to protect me from everyone and everything that had ever hurt me. He often had deep conversations with my dad that lasted for hours. He sought my father's approval for everything concerning me. My father allowed me to move out at the age of seventeen, provided that the apartment passed all inspections, TQ had money in the bank, and had the ability to provide for us. The apartment needed to be clean, and the electricity had to be turned on before I arrived. When I learned that they had given their approval for me to move in with TQ, I was beside myself with excitement. Furthermore, I didn't understand why they had readily agreed to

"Dad, mom?" I called them.

"Yes, Mee Mee?" My mom beamed, looking at me.

"Why did you guys allow me to move out before I turned eighteen?" I was baffled by their decision. I knew I wouldn't find rest until I had an answer to my question.

My parents sat down on the sofa and explained several positive aspects to me.

"We are so proud of your many improvements since Tarquin came into your life and we don't want to hinder your progress in any way." I ran to them for a hug. I love my parents so much because their love for me is unconditional.

My parents were overjoyed to finally see me share a genuine smile, especially after many years of witnessing my deep anguish! "We love Tarquin... he makes you happy and if you're happy, we are happy," my dad revealed.

Our first place was a six hundred square foot efficiency located in Wrightstown, New Jersey. Upon entering the front door, to the left, we had our black faux leather pull-out queen couch bed. About four feet from the couch was our kitchenette, which featured a small brown hotel mini fridge with a tiny freezer at the top that could only hold one small pack of chicken. The counter was about five feet long with a tiny sink to the right side of it. The sink was so small that placing two plates, a cup, and a pot would cause it to overflow. On the counter was where we stored our one plug-in burner. To the right of the kitchen was a small bathroom with a stand-up shower. In front of our couch sat a glass coffee table in black and gold, which matched our end tables that held our black and gold lamps. Behind our coffee table was a chest that supported our color television.

Since we both worked at fast food restaurants, we brought home free food daily. We usually preferred KFC over Wendy's because it remained edible the next day. We didn't need a car because our jobs were less than five minutes away on foot. We had a few cans of beans and corn, cereal and Ramen Noodles for days we didn't want to eat fast food. It wasn't much to some, but it belonged to us and we were very happy. We stayed up all night playing video games and talking about our future. Our conversations always focused on achieving more. Our next goal was to move into a "real apartment" that had a living room and a separate bedroom. I received a raise and was making $5.15 an hour and TQ was making $5.25. We were both working full-time which made it easier to save for a bigger place.

After six months, we began transferring our belongings from our efficiency apartment to the front of the building, which had a living room, an eat-in kitchen, a large bathroom, and a separate bedroom. We were excited to move in and get settled. For a few nights we slept on our black leather couch then TQ went to his parent's house to pick up his mattress which we placed on our bedroom floor. It was our little spot and we were young, happy and in love.

At this point, I had officially become a legal adult. I was eighteen, while TQ was nineteen. I was still working at Wendy's, where customers often joked, "Are you Dave's daughter?" or would say, "Wendy works at Wendy's," followed by a playful laugh. Initially, it was amusing, but after a while, it began to irritate me.

One of my favorite meals that TQ brought home for dinner was honey barbecue wings. They were so messy that even a stack of napkins couldn't keep me clean! The wings were paired with coleslaw and potato wedges smothered in ketchup, and for dessert, we enjoyed a delicious chocolate cake with chocolate chips in it. I would eat an entire cake in a single day and sometimes have it for breakfast, which was one of the perks of living on my own. My parents never allowed me to have cake for breakfast; they always emphasized the importance of eating fruits and vegetables every day. As a kid, whenever I asked for a snack, my mom would often respond, "Go get a piece of fruit." So, being able to eat what I wanted, whenever I wanted, was a thrilling experience for me.

TQ and I both worked similar hours, but sometimes I got home before he did. On those days, I practiced playing video games, and one of our favorites was called The Amusement Park. The objective of the game was to buy rides and create an amusement park. We were scored based on the number of people who rode our customized attractions. The more creative the rides, the more children would want to ride them. The prices for the rides were displayed at the bottom of the TV screen. We played until early the next morning, got a few hours of sleep, and then headed off to work. Those were the days when you could stay up all night, get only a few hours of sleep, and still work all day without feeling cranky or tired. Back then, you didn't even need coffee to perform your job at your best.

Now that we finally had a real kitchen, we needed a dining set. After saving our money, we walked down the hill to a retail store called Aames. We were looking for a black and gold dining room set but ended up settling for a hunter green and gold one, as it was the only style we liked. We loaded the dinette into a shopping cart and then pushed the cart up the steep hill, a distance of about three miles, until we reached our home. We were proud to be so young with a nice, fully furnished apartment. We worked hard for everything we achieved and continued to share our hopes, dreams and plans of our future.

I missed my cycle, so I took a pregnancy test! Surprise! I was pregnant! I was petrified to tell my mother despite having my own place, being employed and being an engaged, legal adult. We didn't have a phone at our place, so I asked my friend, Amy from Wendy's if I could use hers. We sat on her couch for hours rehearsing what I should say. Amy continued to give me pep talks while holding me tight in her arms. I braced myself and picked up the phone. I held the phone to my ear with one hand and my other hand was squeezing Amy's hand so tightly it turned as red as a tomato. I was so afraid of disappointing my family. The phone rang twice before my mom picked up in her sweet, soothing voice. I braced myself and prepared to say the words that she told me that she never wanted to hear.

"Mom, I'm pregnant!"

Then I began to cry. Anytime I went outside as a teen, while living in her house, she would leave me with two phrases. One was, "Why buy the cow if you can get the milk for free!" This meant that I better not be having sex, and the second phrase was, "You better not come home pregnant!" Which meant I better not be having sex PERIOD!

She said those two phrases to me well before sex even crossed my mind. It was her phrases that helped me to hold out as long as I did. While crying hysterically, my mother offered the most reassuring and calming words: she wasn't mad or disappointed.

"Why are you crying, Mee Mee?" she surprisingly asked me.

I blew my nose and hiccupped. "Mom, aren't you disappointed in me?" I asked her.

"I love you Mee Mee, never forget that and never doubt that." I nodded, while holding the phone as if she could see me. "Stop crying, baby; everything will be okay." Again, I nodded, feeling much better. At least she wasn't disappointed in me.

"I am so happy for you, baby," she said, and I could tell that she was smiling. She was happy!

"Will Daddy be mad at me for getting pregnant?" I finally managed to muster up the courage to ask her.

"Everything will be just fine," she reassured me.

My mom assured me that she and Dad had complete faith in Tarquin to take care of both the baby and me. I was eighteen years old and pregnant, and even though I was a legal adult, I still felt like a kid at heart. I was grateful to have already earned my diploma, so my pregnancy wouldn't interfere with my education. While I was scared, I knew I had my mom's support, which gave me confidence that everything would work out. Mom had successfully raised three children, and we all turned out okay, so I felt certain she would be able to guide me in raising my own baby.

I felt relieved when I ended the call and even a little excited. Next, it was time to tell TQ's mom. I was more afraid to tell his mom, especially because she didn't care for me much at first. She is a Southern woman who was very protective of her children. She didn't like any of the girls who lingered around the house for her sons. Now, looking back, I don't blame her; I'm also very protective of my son. She commonly referred to all the little girls in the neighborhood as "scabs" or "sals." I was even more anxious about telling her that I was pregnant. TQ seemed a bit nervous too, which only heightened my anxiety because he was usually so calm, cool, and fearless.

She assisted us with errands, taking us to the grocery store and other necessary locations. On weekends, she would pick us up to do our laundry at her house on McGuire AFB, which is only a few minutes away from our home in Wrightstown.

After several minutes of whispering and contemplating in the back of her gold minivan, where an African head dangled from the rear-view mirror, we finally decided to speak up. To our surprise, she already knew. I had shared my pregnancy with a colleague, and she ended up telling her, even though I had specifically asked her not to. Either way, she knew I was pregnant, and she was also happy! Sharing the news with our mothers wasn't half as bad as we thought it would be.

TQ and I began planning for our new baby. I was determined to be a good mommy, but I worried about my lack of experience. My anxiety about motherhood grew stronger each day. While I was pregnant, TQ and I moved to a nicer apartment in a development called Maple Wood, Apartment, D6. Throughout my pregnancy, TQ was there for me, always accompanying me on my antenatal visits to the hospital. I will never forget everything he did for me and how hard he worked to ensure I felt comfortable. My parents trusted him, and I realize that, like me, they saw that he stood out from the crowd and that he is a good man.

Nine months into my pregnancy, I was experiencing severe cramping, so I called my mother in a panic. I told her that I peed all over myself. She instructed me to smell it and let her know if it smelled like urine, which it didn't. She then realized that my water had broken and told me to call an ambulance, assuring me that she would meet me at the hospital. The ambulance quickly arrived, and before I knew it, I was in the back of the truck, crying for TQ to get in with me.

Prince Tarquan was born in March, fifteen days before his due date. When I discovered that I was pregnant, TQ and I agreed that if we had a boy, his name would be Tarquan, which differs by only one letter from TQ's name, Tarquin. TQ was eager to have a son and often spoke for hours about "his son" before we knew the sex of our baby. On the evening of March 21st, my water broke, and eleven hours later, at 3:00 AM, my "reason" was born at Memorial Hospital, room 315. My precious angel weighed six pounds and eleven ounces. When he was born, his skin was very pale. He had jet-black, cork-silk hair and gray eyes. The moment I looked upon my blessing From God, I was overcome with emotion. I cried as I held him securely to my chest. He was slimy, yet so beautiful. I was a mom, and I vowed to protect and love him with everything I have inside of me.

During the early stages of motherhood, I experienced postpartum depression. I often wondered how I was supposed to raise a baby when I still felt like a child myself. He was so tiny, and I was terrified that I might accidentally hurt him or break him or something. I checked on him multiple times while he slept, watching his chest move up and down. If I didn't see enough movement, I would gently wiggle his arm or leg and wait for a reaction. I stared at him while he slept, curious about what he might be dreaming. My son means the world to me; he is the most important person in my life.

I was so protective of him that I put him in his chair and placed it on the bathroom floor while I used the toilet. I even held him in one arm while I vacuumed the rug with the other. I never wanted to put him down or take my eyes off him. He was so precious and completely mine. I remember praying to God day and night, asking Him to remove all the pain I felt inside.

When "The Prince" was born, I finally felt like I was enough. I felt like I had a true friend who loved me unconditionally, someone who would love me forever. As time progressed, the pain of my past lessened. The feeling of not wanting to live in this world lessened. The visions of being in a car accident or someone killing me because I was unworthy to breathe lessened. Although I never attempted suicide, the thought of what it would be like if someone killed me lessened. I finally felt like I had a purpose, a reason to live... a reason to be something or somebody. One of the best times of my life was when my son was born. I continue to cherish every moment that The Most High grants us together.

I had complete trust in both my parents and TQ's parents regarding watching The Prince, but he only spent the night at my parent's house once while he was a baby. I wanted to be the one to take care of him. It was my responsibility. No one in this world could possibly love him more than his father and me. Once he was born, I had no desire to hang out with friends; I invested every second into ensuring he was protected and happy and that he had opportunities far beyond what I experienced. The peak of my anxiety as a young adult occurred just a few days before my son's first day of preschool. I wasn't ready to let him go, even for just three hours a day. However, I knew he would develop social skills and make friends, so I registered him for school when he turned three. On his first day, TQ and I woke up very early to prepare. I dressed Quan and placed his snack and juice in his little lunchbox.

A few weeks before the school year started, I called

the school to ensure they had my correct address on file, even though I had already received a letter with my son's teacher's name and classroom number. The day before Quan's first day, I called again to express my concerns about him riding the bus. The kind woman on the other end of the line reassured me that he would be safer on a school bus than in my car. She explained that drivers tend to slow down and pay more attention to school buses than to other vehicles. Overwhelmed with emotion, I found myself crying on the phone to a complete stranger. God gave me this precious, perfect child and all I wanted to do was protect him from everyone and anything that could possibly hurt him. After the lady on the phone convinced me that he would be okay, I calmed down a tad, just to get myself worked up a few hours later.

I started my dad's silver minivan with tears in my eyes while I waited with Quan and TQ for the bus to arrive. When the bus arrived, I quickly ran behind it and wrote down the license plate number. After I recorded the tag number in my notebook, I put Quan on the bus and buckled him in. I then hopped in the van with TQ and followed the bus. Each time the bus stopped I frantically wrote the cross streets down in my notebook.

About thirty minutes later, the bus pulled up to the school. I quickly parked, jogged to Quan's bus and stood outside waiting for him to be let out. I had to be there to walk him in his classroom for the first time. Quan was a little nervous but more excited about the opportunity to interact with other children his age. I walked him into his class, where he immediately made himself at home. After about fifteen minutes, his teacher announced that it was time for the parents to leave. She turned his back towards me and gestured for me to exit, but I simply couldn't move. It felt as if my feet were glued to the floor. Who did she think she was to tell me to leave? He was just a baby... my baby! I wasn't ready to leave... Since I couldn't seem to get the hint she came up to me and had very directly told me that it was time for me to go. She said it was best to leave while he was distracted instead of allowing him to see me walk out the door. I still didn't listen. I didn't know her, and I sure didn't trust her with my baby! I didn't care that she had been a teacher for over thirty-two years. She was still a stranger and would have to work hard to earn my trust. Time continued, and she approached me for the third time and said it is time for her to start her class and I needed to leave. I was the only parent remaining. I mustered up enough strength to walk out the door while Quan was playing, but he saw me and began to cry. I turned back to grab him, but the teacher gently nudged me out the door. She told me that everything would be okay and promised me she would take care of him.

I sat outside his classroom for about ten minutes until TQ picked me up from the floor and told me it was time to go home. This was the first time I had been away from him, except for the one night he spent at my parents' house. I ended up driving there around 1:00 AM to pick him up because I couldn't sleep without him.

After about an hour of pacing at home, I couldn't calm my nerves, so I called the school and told them it was an emergency, and that I had to speak to my son immediately. The front desk staff knew who I was. They probably spoke about how nuts I was, but I didn't care. I needed to talk to my son! The secretary told me that she was not able to have Quan pick up the phone because he was busy in class. This lady sounded a little older than the last person and was a bit more patient. She reassured me that he would be okay for three hours.

Two hours passed, and I drove back up to the school. I anxiously sat in the van for about forty-five minutes, then stood outside of his classroom fifteen minutes before dismissal. The staff made an exception to allow me to stand outside of his class and look in if I promised not to interrupt. I quietly observed Quan interact with the other children; He was happy and safe, which made me feel so good inside. Class was over, and I was the first parent to walk in, although we were supposed to wait outside. Quan was happy to see me!

When we got home, he talked about how much fun he had and how he couldn't wait to go back to play with the kids. Each day got a little easier for me, but I didn't fully relax with his teacher until it was towards the end of the school year. When school was out for the summer, I got myself all worked up again. I finally trusted his teacher, but he would have a new teacher the following year. I made her promise to check on him, and she did. The following year, I didn't write the license plate number down, nor did I list every bus stop on my notepad. Each year, he became more independent. I was proud of him.

I had an opportunity to stay at home with Quan until he was about three, while TQ worked multiple jobs to support the household. We didn't earn a lot of money, but it was enough to cover our needs. Since we didn't have our own car yet, TQ rode his silver and red BMX bike, which I had bought for him from Aames. Many days, he rode his bike in the rain, but he never complained. He always said, "I'm going to work hard for my family." He wanted me to stay home and take care of Pooky, and I truly enjoyed being a stay-at-home mother. Our favorite bedtime story was a Little Golden Book titled "The Poky Little Puppy," which now sits on my bookshelf in mint condition. TQ exemplified how a man should care for his family.

After returning to work, we managed to save enough money to buy a car. While choosing our weekend movies at A to Z Video, we came across a light blue 1980 Granada Monarch for sale for seven hundred dollars. We went to the bank, depleted our savings, and purchased our second car. Our first car was a burgundy Ford Escort, which I purchased while catching a ride home from my parent's house. It was priced at three hundred dollars and was sitting in front of a gas station. I paid the man three hundred dollars in cash and was able to take the car, but I still needed a license plate. I asked the owner for permission to search his junkyard for a plate, and he agreed, providing me with a screwdriver. I removed a tag from an old 1970s truck and attached it to the back of my car. The license plate had the word "truck" etched into the bottom, but I didn't mind. It was a license plate, and it was good enough for me. Our radio didn't work, so we sat a boombox in the backseat and drove our car without license, registration or insurance until it died three months later. We removed our belongings and left it in the parking lot in front of the China Dragon Restaurant in Wrightstown.

The Granada was a huge step up from what we had. TQ shined that car for hours. He also hooked up woofers, bought rims and a nice steering wheel cover. We placed Quan's car seat in the back and off we went.

It was a lovely scene and we enjoyed every second of it.

CHAPTER SEVEN

Faith Through Works

TQ and I gave every ounce of love that we have inside ourselves to our son. He received the best of everything we could offer. We both worked extremely hard to ensure that Quan attended a blue-ribbon school and that he was always protected and loved. I signed up for school field trips and volunteered in the lunchroom as much as possible. I took every opportunity to be close to my son. Once he started middle school, he no longer allowed it. I was no longer welcome to walk him to the bus stop. He reached the age when mom being around wasn't cool anymore. He would even walk ahead of me and pretend not to know me if we encountered his friends while shopping at the mall. I always tried to put on a brave face and told him I was proud of his maturity in walking to school by himself. I made an effort to hide my overprotective tendencies from him as much as possible.

The day he told me that I could no longer walk him to the bus, I watched him from his bedroom window as far as I could. I felt a mix of sadness and pride in his growing independence. It was time for me to take a step back and allow his father to teach him how to become a man.

He graduated from high school and is currently attending college, where he has straight A's. He is a responsible young man with a decent income and a car that he has already paid off. Even though he is grown, I still feel excited when he comes home from work or school to share the details of his day. During my pregnancy,

I was very diligent about my health. I made sure to eat plenty of fruits and vegetables, took my prenatal vitamins, and attended all of my doctor appointments.

I was determined to do everything possible to ensure that I had a happy and healthy baby.

I'm so grateful to God for blessing me with my greatest gift, Tarquan.

TQ was incredible during my entire pregnancy. He borrowed my parents' van to drive me to all of my doctor appointments and held my hand every step of the way. While I was pregnant with Quan, I read him stories, sang him songs, and expressed how much I love him. I shared how much I couldn't wait to meet him face-to-face.

Once I delivered him, I made a point to speak "life into him" often. The world is cruel and harsh sometimes. I wanted him to know that despite anything that someone may tell him, he is destined for greatness. Every single day I told him that he is handsome, smart, caring and capable of achieving amazing things. I told him that one day he would be a magnificent father and husband. I never spoke down to him, even when he made mistakes. I never became frustrated or angry, even during those nights when he wouldn't stop crying as a baby. I was always so grateful to have him and will forever be!

I thank God for him every day, and I will continue to do so for a lifetime. My son, The Prince, has given me purpose, and I am eternally grateful for him. He is the most important person in the world. I gave him life, but he has also given me life. He is now twenty-one, and I couldn't be prouder. He is becoming everything I envisioned for him since the day I found out I was pregnant. He is caring, well-mannered, articulate, and so much more. When the time comes, he will be a wonderful father and husband. He pays for college monthly by working a part-time job, and my boy has no debt! I am incredibly proud of him. My greatest prayer is that one day he will realize just how amazing he truly is.

When money was tight, TQ and I would take Quan's old clothes to a child's consignment shop called the Resale Rack located on Route 38 in Hainesport. The owner, an older woman, purchased gently used children's clothes and toys. TQ and I both worked very hard to make ends meet, but some months were harder than others. We made enough money to pay our bills, but we didn't always have a whole lot left over. Thanksgiving was right around the corner and we didn't have enough money for a special dinner, so I did what I knew best. I rummaged through Quan's clothes and toys that he had outgrown, threw them in a trash bag and headed to the Resale Rack. I desperately dumped two large bags across the counter, hoping and praying to receive enough money to buy food for Thanksgiving dinner. Each time the owner quoted a price for an item I shared why the item was worth more than she was offering. She only raised the original quote by a few dollars on rare occasions. For shirts, jackets, and pants, she offered two to three dollars, while for snow suits and electronic toys, the offer was about five dollars. I was just grateful to receive something for items that I knew I would eventually end up giving away for free. After about thirty minutes of reviewing my items and negotiating for more, I walked out with thirty-seven dollars—just enough for Thanksgiving dinner. I put the money in my purse and drove across the street to Giant to buy the necessary items. I looked for sales and was able to purchase everything I needed for thirty-seven dollars, plus a handful of change I found at the bottom of my purse.

A few years ago, I was in Jersey and drove passed the Resale Rack just to share this very story with the owner, but the place was closed. That Resale Rack not only helped with Thanksgiving but also assisted my family and I through a few challenging times. I pray that she lived a prosperous life.

TQ and I became very serious quickly. He was seventeen, and I was sixteen when we first started dating. In just over a year, we were living together as if we were adults. There is nothing quite like young love, where you grow up with your partner and truly get to know them inside and out. You learn how they think, how they feel, and even what they are about to say before they say it. Because our relationship became serious so quickly, we didn't give ourselves the opportunity to grow as individuals. As a result, we decided to take a short break. During this time apart, we committed to spending holidays and birthdays together as a family. We lived in separate homes, but both spent equal time with our son. TQ remained dedicated to his son, even when we weren't living under the same roof full-time. While we were living in separate homes, managing my expenses on just my income was quite challenging. Although TQ contributed financially, his entire contribution went directly to our son, which was immensely helpful for covering Quan's expenses. Unfortunately, this left me struggling to pay for everything else. To make ends meet, I took on three jobs: one at Subway, another at Family Dollar, and a position at a local bank. My dad set a great example by working hard to provide for our family. I didn't want my son to suffer or go without the things that he was used to, just because his father and I took a break.

When I wanted to rekindle my relationship with TQ, I turned to God in prayer. I cleared out half of my closets, expecting that he would soon return and would need the extra space. I also slept on one side of my bed to make room for him. I've always believed in exercising my faith through works—speaking things into existence and living with the expectation that what I desire is on its way. Every time I exercised my faith through action, the desires of my heart became a reality. After a brief separation, we decided to give our relationship another shot. This time, we agreed to allow each other to be our own individuals, in addition to being partners. We also committed to ensuring that God is the foundation and the final arbitrator of everything we do. We refer to the Word (the Holy Bible) regarding all matters that affect our family. This time, we are stronger than ever. We learned a lot about ourselves during our time apart and have developed a deeper understanding and appreciation for one another. We are equally yoked and will continue on our path of love, grace, and individuality.

We will follow the order of priorities outlined in The Word (1 Cor. 11:3):

The Most High, Christ, Husband, Wife, Children. During my split with TQ, I transitioned to Pennsylvania from Jersey. I rented a three-bedroom apartment in Chester. The Landlord called it Trainer, but to me it was all the same. My goal was to move to West Chester in order to be closer to my family. I thought Chester was similar, but to my surprise, it was nothing like West Chester.

I signed the lease for a spacious three-bedroom, one-bath apartment with a washer and dryer hook-up.

The place had brand-new carpets and fresh paint throughout, making it very nice inside. Best of all, it was half the price of my condo in Logan Township, so I moved across the Commodore Barry Bridge. I was relieved that I no longer had to commute from New Jersey to my job in Pennsylvania and pay three dollars each time I crossed the bridge. My new apartment felt much more like a home. After I paid the down payment and reserved a moving truck, I was ready to move in. I was excited to be in Pennsylvania and closer to my parents.

My street was usually quiet, but it seemed like there were issues on every other street surrounding me. I occupied the entire bottom level of the apartment building. Above me lived a woman and her son. On the right side of my building, there was an older gentleman, and directly across from me lived a young couple.

I usually kept to myself when I was at my sanctuary. I would say hello to let others know I was friendly, but I had no intention of making friends or allowing anyone into my home where my son lived. I never hung out outside of my house, nor did I shop in Chester, except for buying iced tea from Crown Chicken. They have the best iced tea I've ever tasted. It has the perfect balance of sweetness with a hint of tartness. No matter how hard Quan and I tried to recreate that flavor at home, we could never get it quite right. Every morning, I woke up early to clean my front porch and sidewalk. No matter how thoroughly I cleaned, I would always find hair weave, empty alcohol bottles, and condoms outside my door. There wasn't a single day when I could wake up to find my front porch as I had left it.

After I cleaned up the trash, I watered my flowers. Outside each of my windows, there were large rectangular hanging pots filled with Rose Mallows, Petunias, Coneflowers, and Marigolds. I had flowers in every color of the rainbow to brighten the neighborhood. Additionally, I placed large clay pots of yellow daisies on my stoop. I was grateful that although I would wake up each morning to trash and other unwanted items, no one disturbed my flowers. My flowers were the only bright thing that I looked forward to seeing each morning while leaving for work and when I pulled up to my house after a long day. They brightened both my day and night and offered others hope.

My neighbors shared how much they looked forward to seeing the flowers, which encouraged me to continue to add my special little touches to brighten our world.

Each night, I envisioned my son attending a blue-ribbon school in West Chester where he would be happy and safe.

On my commute to work, I passed a three-story grey townhome. I pondered on what the inside might look like. I imagined how I would decorate it and what it would feel like to live in West Chester again. I decided to activate my faith, so I pulled up to the very townhome that I drove past each morning. I then said, "God, I thank you for my new home in the name of Jesus." A few weeks after pulling into the driveway, I decided to expand my faith by not only pulling into the driveway but getting out of my car, walking to the front door, and turning the doorknob to truly experience what it felt like to be in my new space. Thank goodness no one saw me turning someone's door knob and decided to call the police, thinking I was breaking in.

About three months later, the landlord of the grey townhome approached me while I was sitting at my desk at work. He said

"I heard you were looking for a place for you and your baby."

I looked into the man's dark eyes and smiled. The man smiled back, and I responded by saying, "Yes." The man stared at me again for what seemed like forever as if deciding if he really wanted me to be a tenant in his house.

"Here's a key. Why don't you drive over and take a look at it when you are less busy?"

I was surprised as I hadn't expected this moment. In the man's hand, there was a key. I reached for it, took it into my palms, and stared at it in wonder.

"Just take a look at the house and get back to me as soon as you can," he told me with a smile on his face. I called my current Landlord in Chester and requested to break my lease.

"You wanna' break your lease?" he asked me, sounding surprised since I was only living in Chester for a few months.

"Yes, I wanna' break my lease as soon as possible," I replied over the phone.

"Well, I have no issues with you, and I see no reason why your lease shouldn't be broken if you want it to," he responded.

"Thank you." He seemed like a genuinely understanding and supportive person.

"I'm glad you found a home that makes you happier. You were a great tenant." I smiled to myself, then replied, "Thank you for being an awesome landlord."

"Well, I wish you the best, dear. Actually, I really enjoyed having you around," he declared, and I inwardly smiled again.

"Thank you for having me," I responded.

"By the way, if you need a reference, I would be

glad to give you one," the man supplied, and at that moment, my heart softened and a sense of gladness filled me. I was glad he chose to be understanding when I told him I wanted to break my lease. Some landlords might have caused a scene or made a fuss, but he seemed to have no time for that.

"I will keep that in mind... you will be the first person I contact when I need a reference," I assured him.

"Well, if that is it, miss, enjoy the rest of your day," he said on the other side of the line.

"You too, Ryan," I said before the line disconnected. I couldn't believe my good fortune. Finally, I would get the house of my dreams and my little prince would attend a blue-ribbon school. I packed my things and off I went, headed to my new place in West Chester.

It was even more beautiful than I had imagined! My son was going to a blue-ribbon school, and the home was spectacular! When I entered the garage, I discovered a small basement area with a door leading to a charming fenced backyard. Above the finished basement was the living room, featuring a fireplace and a partial bathroom. The nice-sized kitchen had laminate floors and wood cabinets, along with an extra bedroom that I converted into a dining room. Directly above the living room was my bedroom, a full bathroom, and a closet with a stackable washer and dryer, conveniently located next to my son's room.

The home was freshly painted with brand new neutral rugs. It was stunning and felt like home! I praised God every step of the way.

I heard about college and I saw it on TV... After years of wondering what college would be like if I attended, I mustered up enough courage to register at a community college close to home. My major was Early Childhood Education. I started by taking English and Math. I chose to begin with those subjects because I was naturally good at English, so I liked it a tad and I sucked at math. I thought it would be a good idea to balance one subject that I am strong in and one subject that I am weak in. I started with art because I figured that all I would need to do was draw, but I was wrong.

Attending college was overwhelming at first. In math class, the professor would swiftly write down equations on the board that could not be found in our three-hundred-dollar math book. He would then quickly provide instructions then erase the board just to write down the next set of equations. By the time I was halfway finished writing the information in my notebook, he would begin erasing the board all over again. No matter how fast I wrote, I just couldn't keep up with him. I was lagging in taking notes and the tasks were foreign to me. When I raised my hand for further clarification, he quickly rambled the answer, turned his back to me and continued what he was doing. After class one day, I expressed my concern to him. I waited until most students had exited, and when I noticed the lecture hall was nearly empty, I packed my books and hurried toward the man.

"Good morning Professor Jackson," I said while smiling.

"Good morning to you as well. How can I help you?" he asked, looking at me without any surprise. I suppose they receive so many questions from students after class that they become accustomed to it.

"Sir, I'm falling behind in your class. Most times, you erase the board before I can copy down what you've written on it," I sadly complained.

His response was, "keep up or take another class."

Hearing him say that left me speechless. I never expected him to make that remark. After all, he was a teacher, and I assumed he would offer me some advice on how to catch up with him and the other students. It turned out I was mistaken, which left me feeling dejected.

"Whether you pass or fail, I still get paid," he told me without shame. I could do nothing more than just stare at him with eyes wide open.

He showed no empathy or concern for my feelings, nor did he care that I was trying to catch up with him in class. I believe he hated everything about his job, including his students. His cold demeanor wasn't directed only at me; he treated everyone this way. I was always on time, respectful, and I participated as much as possible, but it didn't earn me extra brownie points with the professor. I even sat in the front row to demonstrate engagement, but he couldn't care less. Talking to him about my struggles in his class was no help. After a while, I realized that I wasn't the only student left behind. There were many of us in this situation. In fact, I can confidently say that more than half the class was struggling, and the professor seemed indifferent. This experience made me realize that I was no longer in high school; I was now in college. To succeed and survive; I needed to work extra hard.

After careful consideration, I decided to partner with another student who was facing similar challenges. Her name is Ann. "I'm really falling behind in Professor Jackson's class," I admitted one morning during class. "You're not alone in this. I'm struggling too," Ann replied.

"Why don't we partner?" I asked her, and she readily

agreed. From then on, we became partners and things became a little simpler for us. I focused on only writing the first side of the dry-erase board, and she focused on the second side. After class, we would exchange notes, getting the opposite half of what we had written down. I felt empowered! Instead of allowing him to win and break my spirit by showing absolutely no regard for my commitment to learning, I fought back! I aced his class after strategizing, putting in extra time and taking advantage of tons of tutoring! In art, silly me... I thought that if I drew pictures and painted, I would ace that class. I had no idea that the art class that I registered for had absolutely nothing to do with that. It was the study of many well-known artists such as Vincent Van Gosh, Picasso and Leonardo da Vinci. I should have taken the time to review the syllabus prior to registering.

I needed to know everything there was to possibly know about the style of art along with the history of each artist. However, once I realized how much work was involved in math alone, I dropped my English class and planned to pick it back up later since I knew I could easily catch up. It was time for my mid-semester check-in. I was thrilled about discussing my future as a college student with one of their trusted advisors. I never thought that I would have graduated high school with a diploma. Now, here I am in college, about to meet with a real advisor. I shared all my hopes, dreams and aspirations with the advisor. I poured every bit of my heart on his table. I thought he would provide all the answers to my many questions about college life. I shared my strong aspirations of being a teacher since the age of four and how I loved playing school as a child. Grading papers was my favorite part, especially when I was able to list their grades with my red crayon or reward hard work with stickers. I even got a kick out of marking papers with F's because it made me feel so official.

Throughout my interaction with the advisor, I spoke with enthusiasm and passion, while he only responded with words of confusion and discouragement. He, just like my math professor, showed no true concern for me or my future. I felt like I was wasting his time. His words stayed with me as I walked through the long halls back to my car.

"If you get a degree in education, you will need to spend two to four years in college or maybe even longer and after all the money you spend, along with your time and hard work, you will only make about thirty grand a year."

My advisor's words captivated me for several moments. I felt confused and disappointed that I had nothing more to share with him. As I looked into the man's cold eyes, I realized that I needed to reflect on my life before making a decision about whether to continue with college.

I couldn't shake his discouraging words from my mind. After completing the semester, I decided to drop out of college. What was the point of spending all that time and money just to earn thirty grand? I knew I could make that amount, or even more, through hard work and determination. So, that became my plan moving forward.

CHAPTER EIGHT

Movin' & Shakin'

As a retail assistant manager, I was responsible for greeting customers, creating floor models and clothing displays, and handling cashier and stock duties. Ever since my first job at Wendy's as a teenager, I have held leadership positions. Each evening, I would count down the registers, fill out the business deposit forms, and place the money and checks in a sealed plastic bag for the next morning's drop-off at the bank, which was directly across the street from my workplace. Every time I entered the bank, I found myself fantasizing about being a bank teller. The atmosphere was much more professional than my own. The staff were friendlier, and the environment was clean. I imagined how I would look in a sweater vest featuring their logo on the upper left side of the shirt.

I hated my retail job because not only did the hours suck, but I worked alongside another assistant manager who made my life a living hell! She was the same age as my mother, so I expected a higher level of maturity.

Mrs. Latoya went out of her way to bring me down every chance she got. She would often say, "Wendy, you're really not happy; I don't know why you pretend so much." I was never boastful or frowned upon anyone, so I wasn't sure where she got the idea that I was pretending. I was, in fact, very blissful because each day, I would reflect on the days when I hated myself and didn't want to get out of bed. I often thought about the days I feared someone killing me because I was unworthy of breathing. Yes!!! I was ecstatic that I didn't have those feelings anymore. I was thankful that I didn't have night terrors.

Despite all the heartache and pain I endured, I generally have a happy-go-lucky attitude. I feel truly blessed to have a loving husband and a son who brings me joy. Most importantly, I know that God loves me, and that's really all I need. It doesn't take much to make me happy; even the little things can bring a smile to my face. This is especially meaningful to me since there was a time when I never smiled at all.

I always arrive at work thirty minutes early to give myself time to mentally unwind. I don't like to pull up, hop out of my car the moment I park, and immediately step into the building. Taking this time to mentally plan my day and think clearly without distractions boosts my confidence, which in turn increases my productivity.

The days I was scheduled with Mrs. Latoya, I literally gave myself exactly fifty seconds to walk from my car to the time clock. I couldn't bear to be around her, not a minute too long or a minute too soon. I was about 5'3", weighing one hundred pounds while Mrs. Latoya stood at 5'11" and weighed three hundred fifty pounds, which made her a bit intimidating. When she spoke to me condescendingly, I did my best to ignore her. She stood at the register, eating potato chips while ringing up customers who seemed too afraid to mention the crumbs landing on their clothes. Whenever she needed assistance, she yelled across the room, and since I was committed to helping customers, I would rush to her aid. I tried my best to stay positive despite her daily ridicule and torment.

Her constant remarks regarding me not really being happy, coupled with her condescending tone any time she spoke to me, not to mention how she rolled her eyes each time we had conversations, caused me to even doubt my own happiness. She slowly started to bring me back to that dark place. I started to question myself "maybe I'm not really happy?" "Maybe my life really does in fact suck?" Before I knew it, I handed over the power that I worked so very hard to acquire to her. Things became so unpleasant working with her that I would sit in my car and cry prior to my shift on the days that I had to work with her. When I was finished bawling my eyes out, I cleaned up my face and put on some lip gloss and proceeded with my day. As I look back over this situation, I realize that people who are hurt are already going through a tough ordeal, and only a few people notice that. I also realized that hurt people tend to want to hurt others. I finally came to the conclusion that the words that she was saying to me were words that she was most likely saying to herself. She was married with a son whom she always bragged about, but she seemed so miserable. If someone goes out of their way to try to hurt you for being happy, it says more about them than it does about you. I prayed long and hard about the situation at work. I told God that I didn't want to work with Mrs. Latoya anymore. I cried many days in my car before walking in the door to work and cried myself to sleep many nights dreading working with her the next day.

One day, after drying my tears in my car and gathering myself to face Mrs. Latoya's torment, I discovered she wasn't there. She was scheduled to close with me, but when I arrived, I found out that she had been terminated and was now working at a different retail store up the road. The news that she would no longer be working with me brought a greater sense of peace. However, I still found myself fantasizing about having a bank job. During some nights in the holiday season, I wouldn't get home until 11:00 PM or later.

The bank closed at 3:00 PM and was closed on Sundays. After over a year of fantasizing about working at the bank, I decided to apply. I figured I needed to have a college degree, but I had some college education and I managed to maintain a 4.0 GPA. I was ready to give it a shot.

I completed a two-page paper application with blue ink and handed it to a lady sitting at a desk by the entrance. Shortly after I submitted my application, I received a phone call for an interview. I couldn't believe they called me back. On the application I listed that I didn't have a college degree. Maybe they made a mistake; maybe they didn't mean to select my application. There had to be a mix-up. I couldn't understand why they called me. I scheduled the interview the following week. Each day I imagined them saying, "Sorry we made a mistake; we thought you had a college degree."

While patiently waiting for my interview to begin, I replayed all the lies that I was told by others along with all the lies I told myself… "You're stupid." "You're ugly." "You're worthless." My heart was racing so fast that I thought you could see it pounding through my chest and even hear it beating. I wore black slacks creased, as my dad taught me, black flats and a white button-down shirt. It was the best outfit that I had and could afford.

It was time to interview for the position. My palms were sweaty; I wanted to pee so badly. I wondered if he could hear my heart pounding out of my chest because it sounded extra loud to me. Steve asked me several questions, and I answered to the best of my ability while looking down at my feet most of the time. Not sure what was on the floor while he was talking but looking him in his eyes made me more nervous. I couldn't wait until the interview was over; I was starting to squirm in my chair a tad because I had to pee so badly. The interview was over, and I was free to leave. Funny… as soon as I walked out the front door, I didn't have to go to the bathroom anymore. I mentally moved on from the interview because not only did I bomb it, I didn't have a college degree.

Two weeks after the interview, I received a call from the bank recruiter. I braced myself,

"Maybe they also call when you don't get the job?"

I said to myself. I started to mentally prepare for the bad news. There was a three-second pause before she spoke.

"Good morning," the lady on the other side of the line said.

"Good morning," I replied, feeling so very nervous. "Am I speaking with Miss Wendy Massey?" she asked in a soprano voice.

I gulped once and then twice. "Yes, this is Wendy Massey," I answered.

"We'd like to extend a job offer as a bank teller with a starting salary of $8.25 an hour."

Hearing her voice on the other end of the line, I was mesmerized. I had never thought I would be fortunate enough to get that job. I could already envision myself working at the bank. I took a deep breath and smiled. The salary was the same as what I was currently earning as an assistant manager, so I wouldn't be losing any money. At the time, I didn't have the negotiation skills, so I gladly accepted the position. I did it! I landed my dream job! After over a year of fantasizing about being a bank teller, I had finally achieved it!

I successfully completed training and was ready to start my position at a branch conveniently located in a plaza behind my house. Our very first mortgage was on a three-bedroom, two-and-a-half-bath townhome with a fireplace. It had a cute fenced backyard, plenty of children for Quan to play with and was perfect for raising a family. I was living the life that I only dreamed of. I received positive performance reviews at work and was making enough money to get by.

I made a best friend at work. She was another mommy with a son around the same age as mine. I loved having Mommy talk with her and scheduling play dates. She always came to my house with the most thoughtful, creative gifts. In her special bags, I would find homemade chocolate chip cookies (my favorite), candles and hand-written coupons for a free house cleaning, babysitting or home-cooked meals. She showed me that you don't need a lot of money to be thoughtful or happy. I enjoyed her company and her level of simplicity and humility. We were inseparable. Our manager, who was a few years older than us, didn't seem to appreciate our happiness and camaraderie. We didn't care much about her opinion because we had each other. When my best friend became pregnant with her daughter, she decided to leave the company to focus on her family.

"Are you really leaving?" I asked. I couldn't remember ever caring for anyone I'd worked with like I cared for her. It was like I knew her forever.

"I have to leave, Wendy. I am carrying my second

child and I don't think I can cope with both work and pregnancy at the same time."

I nodded at her. I remembered the discomfort I felt when I was carrying my baby and knew that she was also going through the same, or maybe worse.

"I will miss you." To my surprise, I felt a lump in my throat.

She smiled at me, embraced me and then looked at me. Her hands cupped my small face in her hands. "I'll miss you more, Wendy. I'm glad I met you."

I shrugged, trying to get hold of the tears threatening to run down my cheeks.

"I am so glad I met you too," I replied with a forced smile.

"Wendy, how bout' we keep in touch even after I'm gone?" she suggested.

I nodded my head. "That would be a good idea. We should keep in touch." I agreed to her suggestion. As she turned to leave, I felt empty, sad and alone. I didn't realize I had grown so attached to her until she was gone. The first few weeks were terrible. I would turn towards where she normally sat and then feel like I lost something. Even though we stayed in touch, work just wasn't the same without her. Once she was gone, I didn't have anyone to lean on when my supervisor gave me a hard time.

I always extended grace to my supervisor because she was going through personal challenges at home and had a health condition. I could only imagine how tough her life was, so when she was mean and cranky, which was most of the time, I tried to empathize. She went out of her way, just like Mrs. Latoya, to try to bring me down.

Her favorite phrase to me was "You're nothing, and you will never be anything, and don't you ever forget that." I was proud of my accomplishments, so I walked with my head held high. I was loved by my family and overcame things that I thought would kill me, so my level of enthusiasm was higher than most. She thought I was arrogant because I was becoming confident in myself and didn't give her the power to bring me down. She rolled her eyes when having a conversation with me just like Mrs. Latoya, but I was done sitting in my car crying. All the other tellers did exactly what she said and would kiss up to her, but kissing up to people was never my thing. I would naturally ignore her and make a point to only speak to her when necessary in a very professional yet less emotional tone than I offered others.

Because I was the only one who didn't follow her around like a little puppy, telling her how pretty she was, buying her candy or anything else to stroke her ego, she would get annoyed. After several months of her taunting me, especially with my sidekick absent to laugh it off with, I had finally had enough. This time, she got in my face, looked me straight in the eyes, and said, "Wendy, who do you think you are?" She looked upset. I decided to ignore her and walk away, but to my surprise, she stepped in front of me, standing like a soldier ready for battle.

"I'm talking to you. How dare you walk out on me?" she asked. As she talked, I could see that she was angry. Did she really think I would stand by and allow her to bully me? When it was obvious I wasn't going to answer her or retaliate, she looked me into the eyes and said, "You are nothing, Wendy."

"What did you just say?" I asked. Perhaps she didn't see the fire in my eyes.

"You heard me right, girl," she retorted, showing no remorse.

Hearing that, I lost control of the little patience I had left. I knew it was finally time I put her in her place, or else she would keep provoking and taunting me. My face was burning with anger, and without thinking, I stretched out my hands toward her and pushed her hard with all the strength I had in me. I would typically walk away with no response, but getting in my personal space too often put me in defense mode.

I never kissed up to her or anyone else because I don't believe in it. People are people, just like me. Titles and money do not make anyone above or beneath the next person. With her, I just kind of stayed in my own lane. She would taunt me, and I would walk away. Then she would follow me and taunt me some more. I felt like I was in high school all over again. Once she entered my personal space in a threatening manner, one time too many I naturally went into defense mode and pushed her as hard as I could, causing her to fall back and hit the floor hard. It took three strong men to restrain me. I was going to let her have it, but I'm glad I didn't. They broke it up before a real fight happened. She then ran out of the room crying. I was told to leave for the day. Thank God I didn't get written up or fired. I think the branch manager knew she had it coming because he witnessed how she taunted me but never said anything. From that day forward, she never messed with me again. We exchanged "good mornings" and a few words when necessary. After a few weeks, we both got over it and life went on.

As I gained more experience in banking, I became more confident in my abilities. I was always prepared for my next move, so I regularly checked the classifieds for job opportunities, despite being content in my current role. One day, I found a bank teller position at THS Bank, which offered a dollar more per hour than what I was currently earning. I decided to apply. During the interview, I felt much more self-assured. Having already acquired the necessary experience, I was familiar with many of the questions they would ask. I was hired on the spot, and my banking career continued to flourish.

Throughout my banking career, I have held various positions, including Teller, Lead Teller, Banker, Assistant Manager, Service Manager, Branch Manager, and Assistant Vice President. I worked at THS Bank for approximately three years.

Out of nowhere, I decided to pursue a different path and started a career in the fitness industry. My goal was to become a personal trainer, further my education, and potentially own my own gym. Initially, the position seemed promising, but after accounting for all the fees and realizing that the starting salary was even lower than what I earned at THS, I began to face challenges. There was a small incentive offered for enrolling new clients in gym services or upgrading their existing plans. However, if I wasn't successful in making sales during a given month, I found it hard to make ends meet. Additionally, the job required me to work nights, weekends, and all holidays, with mandatory overtime during the holiday season. The recruiter didn't mention any of this during our interview. She made it sound so easy. I gave it a shot and put my best foot forward, but I wasn't making enough money to pay my bills, so I returned to what I knew best: banking. I went to the office where I wanted to work, approached the door, and peered inside. I envisioned myself working at this specific location for this particular company. Although I had experience in bank management, I applied for a position as a banker because I was attending college and wanted a job that wouldn't be too stressful or distract me from my studies. I was working hard and focused on maintaining a 4.0 GPA, which I was very proud of.

At the beginning of the interview, the recruiter looked at us and smiled.

"I welcome you to this interview, but I must say that the time spent in this room may be your only opportunity to shine." She was still smiling while she spoke.

The recruiter was dressed in a pair of black slacks and a white shirt. She appeared very professional. I almost felt intimidated by her, but my experience in the banking sector reassured me.

"I will never know anything about any of you seated here if you don't share it with me," she continued to speak, staring into our eyes. I looked at the woman again, trying to think fast. I knew she was sending us a message. I had to hastily decipher her message and act quickly.

"Finally, I strongly advise you all to participate. Thank you," she said and took her seat. We all stared at her. We had all come from different backgrounds and places for this interview, and only the chosen ones would be given this chance. I desperately wanted this job, as I never wanted to return to working at the gym.

After she sat down, I reflected on what she had said and finally concluded that the recruiter only wanted us to step up and showcase our skills. I was wearing a nice grey suit and had three resumes neatly arranged in a leather folder. I felt like I looked the part. As I surveyed the packed room of about twenty people, I noticed that everyone else looked the part too. Some wore suits that were just as nice as mine, while others sported even better attire. The room was filled with what appeared to be all business professionals. I had hoped to stand out with my sharp appearance, but in terms of looks, I blended in with the crowd. They also had resumes, with some placed in leather folders like mine, while others pulled theirs out of fancy briefcases. I had never considered bringing a fancy briefcase.

Since I blended in based on outward appearance, I decided to rely on my enthusiasm. Although I had been criticized for this trait, it could be the key factor that helps me stand out. If I could balance my enthusiasm with a confident demeanor, perhaps I would have a chance. The interview began with introductions, and the recruiter asked us to share our names and something about ourselves. At that point, I noticed that a quarter of the people who initially seemed very confident now appeared uncertain, just like me. Seizing every opportunity, I raised my hand to answer her questions.

"Share a time when you had a challenging customer interaction? What was the challenge, how did you resolve it, and how did the customer feel?"

I didn't know what I was going to say; I only remembered her saying that it was my only time to shine. I opened my mouth and the answers just flowed. I shared my enthusiasm, my passion for people and tried my best to remain balanced... not too much enthusiasm... not too much confidence. In the middle of the interview, the recruiter asked me to step into the hall. My heart started racing. I couldn't help but think, "What if I was too enthusiastic? What if she was about to tell me those dreaded words I didn't want to hear?"

As I exited what felt like the conference room, I sensed about two dozen pairs of eyes on me. I couldn't help but wonder what I had done or said wrong. I followed her into the hall, and I could already feel my heartbeat racing; it brought back memories of the tension I felt during my first banking interview, which had clouded my memory. Suddenly, the recruiter stopped walking and turned to face me, prompting me to stop as well.

"Thank you for your time. We will contact you if we are interested." were the words I imagined her about to say. I braced myself, mentally encouraging myself as I waited for her to speak.

"If she's not interested, be professional and polite and walk away with your head held high."

I thought to myself.

The recruiter paused and looked at me. She said, "With your experience in bank management, have you ever thought about being an entry-level manager?" I told her that I applied for the banker position because I was in school and wanted to focus on my education, but I would accept the challenge and would be more than happy to apply. I applied and interviewed again, and within two weeks, I was hired as an entry-level manager. I called all the most important people in my life and shared the good news! I finished all my paperwork, background check, and drug test, and I was prepared to officially start training.

When I started my career at Somers Bank, I collected every brochure, magazine, handout, and any other material related to the company that I could find. I spread everything out on my living room floor and read each item daily. I read some in the morning, others in the evening, and even some while I was in the bathroom. Before long, I had memorized our entire development booklet, cover to cover. I learned everything about our CEO, the year Somers was founded, and the company's value. Additionally, I became well-versed in all the products and services we offered. I planned to make this my last stop, so I wanted to invest in my future. I believed that the more I learned, the faster I would advance. Each time the lead manager visited our branch, I made it a point to talk to him. I would ask him what I needed to do to get promoted. He would respond by setting an extremely challenging, almost impossible goal for me, and each time, I exceeded those expectations. No matter what challenge he presented, I dedicated extra time to surpass it. While most people were working forty hours a week, I was putting in fifty-five hours, seven days a week. I was willing and determined to do whatever it took to refine my skills.

When my lead manager left the company, I followed the same process, dedicating extra time to exceed expectations with his replacement. I didn't skip a beat. When my office manager, whom I reported directly to, also left, I was asked to step up and lead the team until a new manager was found. I viewed every opportunity as a chance to demonstrate to senior leadership that I was worthy of the crown. I fulfilled all requests, surpassed expectations, and managed my office with minimal supervision and support. When the position became available for application, I applied along with many other long-term employees. However, these other candidates had more connections within the company and possessed more education than I did.

The night before the interview, I looked in my bathroom mirror and said, "My name is Wendy Massey; I am the new Office Manager of the Sunset Street location," which I said three times. I then said, "God, I thank you for my promotion in Jesus name." I also created a removable nameplate to place on top of my current name tag, which read "Wendy Massey, Entry-Level Manager." The new nameplate stated "Wendy Massey, Office Manager." Although I was nervous to wear it, I firmly believe in the power of mind over matter and the strength of faith with works. During the interview, the lead manager asked me why I put the title "Office Manager" over my current role as "Entry-Level Manager." I responded by saying, "I am speaking it into existence." He just looked at me with the best poker face I've ever seen. I wasn't sure if he was pleased or upset.

I continued to answer his questions, but he never revealed how he felt about my responses. I couldn't tell if I was failing or succeeding. He looked deeply into my eyes without showing any emotion as I spoke about my passion for leading and inspiring others. I also mentioned that I had exceeded all of his challenging goals and was performing higher than my peers. After about an hour and a half, the interview concluded.

I shook his hand, thanked him for his time, and exited his office without any sense of how well or poorly I had performed. My mind raced with questions: "What if he thought changing my title on my name tag was arrogant or tacky? What if he misunderstood my projected confidence? What if he considered my name tag unprofessional or silly? What if I didn't answer any of his questions correctly?" So many thoughts flooded my mind. Several weeks passed, and I still hadn't heard back, so I decided to reach out to human resources. They informed me that a decision had not yet been made. I mentally moved on, realizing that with all the connections and education that other candidates had, they were likely to get the position over me. Additionally, I had been with the company for less than a year, which is the standard amount of time required in a role before applying for other positions. About five weeks after my interview, I was preparing for a meeting when the lead manager walked in. I moved on from not getting the position and vowed to secure the next one that came around. The lead manager stared at me for what seemed like ages and I found myself wondering what he was thinking. "Massey?" He called my name, as he looked into his eyes. I didn't know what he was thinking or what I should expect.

"Give me a very good reason why I should hire you."

He was still staring at me.

As soon as I heard him ask me that question, I realized that the moment I had been waiting for had finally arrived. This was my opportunity to either secure the job or lose it. I knew I needed to make a strong impression. My heart began to race, and I had to remind myself to think clearly and carefully before responding. I swallowed, looked him in the eyes, and smiled. While smiling, I quickly considered the best answer to give him.

I never wanted to lose the opportunity for any reason. I expressed my dedication and passion for people and conveyed that I wanted this position more than anything.

As I spoke, the lead manager kept looking at me, never taking his eyes off me as he listened attentively to my explanation. At one point, I saw him nod his head as if in agreement with what I was saying. Finally, when my lips stopped moving, the lead manager smiled at me.

"Massey, you got the job!" I was dumbfounded for a minute or two. At first, I didn't seem to understand what he was saying, and when my brain finally understood, I was overwhelmed with excitement.

"Oh my goodness!" I exclaimed.

I jumped up and down with tears in my eyes which I quickly wiped away before he noticed. I'm sure he didn't expect that, but I was so happy that I couldn't help myself.

"Oh, thank you very much for allowing me an opportunity,

I said, no longer bothering to wipe the hint of tears building up in my eyes.

"You deserve it, Massey. You worked very hard for it." He seemed to remind me.

I beamed at him. "I am so very grateful for this opportunity. I promise to do my best, and I won't let you down," I said.

"I will be counting on that," he said with a smile, putting his hands in his pockets as he casually strolled out of the office. I cried tears of joy during my commute to my next meeting. I couldn't believe that the girl with the lowest self-esteem in the world—the girl who once felt worthless and thought she would never live past the age of twenty-one—was being promoted to office manager after a short time with the company. I thanked God for opening another door and felt thrilled about everything He had in store for me!

"Sometimes you must work harder until you're able to work smarter" — RRS

I felt uneasy while in the presence of the other office managers because they were articulate and seemed to know what they were doing. They appeared to have strong friendships, while I was just a newbie. Their suits were tailored, their shoes polished, and they looked put together. I felt like a baby fish in a tank full of sharks. I only owned one nice grey suit, which was too snug, and the suit my mom had given me.

Being an acting office manager was nothing like the real thing. In meetings, the other managers used terminology I had never encountered before. As they spoke these unfamiliar terms, I quietly observed, trying not to look lost. Before major meetings, I would anticipate every question the facilitator might ask and rehearse the answers that I believed would sound the best. Despite practicing repeatedly, I still lacked confidence and felt as though I just wasn't good enough to stand alongside the other managers.

Each day before going to work, especially before going into a big meeting, I called my mom, who would always lift my spirits. Mom has always been my biggest supporter and cheerleader! No matter what I was going through, she encouraged me to hold my head up. When I had my head down as a little girl, she would gently lift up my chin and say, "always keep your shoulders back and your head up no matter what." Those words give me strength.

My famous words during our conversation were,

"Mom, I'm scared." "They are so much smarter than me." "They know what they are doing," and she would reassure me by saying, "you have what it takes, just keep movin' and shakin' girl." It became my mantra. Each time things became difficult, her words would come to mind, "Shoulders back, head up, keep movin' and shakin'." I thought of her words so much that I created a little jingle called "movin' and shakin'." Anytime I felt overwhelmed, I would think of my mom and sing the jingle until I felt confident. Where I lacked experience or knowledge, I made up with hard work.

My goal was to always work smarter, not harder, but until I got there, I had to work as hard as it took to measure up with my peers. I started to write down all the big, unfamiliar words that I heard in manager meetings. I then went home and researched each word, its definition and how to pronounce it. I practiced using the words in a sentence while interacting with family. I wanted to get practice first because I didn't want to screw it up in front of the people at work. As I continued to use the words that I was once unfamiliar with, I became more confident using them. To enhance my vocabulary, I started studying unfamiliar words and reading the newspaper. Although I wasn't particularly interested in current events, I believed that reading the paper made me appear more intelligent. It also provided me with discussion topics for large meetings and helped broaden my vocabulary. I continued the process—If I didn't know or understand a word in the newspaper, I researched it, found out the meaning, then used it in a sentence starting with my family until I was comfortable using that word at work.

After spending several months with leadership,

I began to pick up the culture naturally without even trying anymore. I was able to somewhat talk the talk, but still couldn't walk the walk. I thought all the other meetings I attended were a big deal, but I had an even bigger meeting scheduled. This meeting was with all the lead managers, office managers, supporting partners and the head of compliance. I still didn't have enough money for a real suit. Most times, I would match a black blazer that I purchased at Deb along with some black slacks I purchased at Boscov's. The shades of black were slightly off, but that was the best I could do. I couldn't wear my "off-black" suit to the huge meeting. I nervously went to my mom's house for assistance. She opened her closet and instructed me to take whatever I wanted. My mom always had my back, no matter what. She took every single call at any time of the day, no matter how busy she was. She especially made herself available during my lunch hour because that was when I needed a pep talk the most...

Okay... back to my story.

I looked in her closet and instantly fell in love with a cream-colored wide-leg pant suit. The shade of cream, the cut of the suit, and the fancy button on the jacket made it look very official. She said I could have it and then began grabbing shoes from the bottom of her closet. Mom was always excited to help me with anything I needed. After pairing my new suit with a nice pair of pumps, she turned to her jewelry box. She reassured me that even though the suit was a little big, it would look perfect on me no matter what. This was going to be my first official suit as an office manager. The cream suit blew my too small grey interview suit out of the water. I was excited to have a beautiful outfit for my big meeting, but I was also nervous because it was much too big. As I tried the suit on, I looked back at my mom, who offered the warmest smile of reassurance. The suit appeared even larger than we had anticipated. My mom picked up my chin and said, "shoulders back, head high, just keep movin' and shakin'." She told me not to worry because the jacket would hide everything.

The next morning, I put on my oversized silk shirt, my oversized suit, my mom's broach, and my grandmother's pearls (RIP), which were near and dear to my mom. The waist of the paint was so large that placing a belt through the hoops caused it to look scrunched up and bulky. No matter how I maneuvered the belt through the loops, nothing seemed to work.

It was just about time to leave for the big meeting, and I didn't have enough time to drive back to my parents' house for help, so I called my dad. It was too early for Mom to be up; I was glad someone answered. I shared my suit concerns with my dad. He told me that everything would be okay. My dad was and continues to be my hero, so if he said it would be okay, then I believed him. Instead of remaining in panic mode, I went into "find a way" mode. I rolled the waistband of the pants down twice and secured the flap with several safety pins. To minimize the bulge, I placed a large gold belt around my waist over the pants. My jacket covered part of the remaining bulge, and the large purse I carried camouflaged the rest. When I felt insecure I simply crossed my arms to my side and then placed my large purse over whatever part of the suit was out of place. Thank God we sat down during most of the meeting. From the waist up, I looked official and was able to blend in with the other managers. The suit was extremely uncomfortable, though. Anytime I moved in my seat it would shift my belt and cause everything to be out of place all over again.

I didn't drink much water because I was hoping not to use the ladies' room during the entire meeting. It took so long to get everything in place that I didn't want to have to fix it all over again, but I couldn't hold it anymore. I had to go... I removed the large gold belt, all six large safety pins, and unrolled the waist twice just to pull my pants down.

Then, I had to put everything back into place. I was so glad that we were on break because it took almost ten minutes just to get everything back in order. When lunch was over, I walked back into the boardroom, sat at the far end of the table and tried my best not to move. The meeting was over.... I did it!! I talked the talk and somewhat walked the walk. I even managed not to poke myself with any pins during the meeting. I shined bright, just like my parents said I would. I got home, told them all about it and went to bed feeling good.

As the weather became colder, I could no longer wear my mother's navy blazer or dress sweaters. I had a little extra money saved up for a professional coat. After paying all my bills, I had fifty dollars left over. I was thrilled to finally have money after paying bills for the first time in a very long time. I had to save gas, so I couldn't go to the mall. The closest store was Kmart. Besides, the last time I went to the mall, the cheapest coat that I could find was priced at ninety dollars. The first thing I looked for when I walked in the doors of Kmart was the clearance rack. I lived on a tight budget, so shopping on clearance or browsing the sale rack was a part of my regular shopping routine.

As I browsed through the coat racks, I noticed that most of the coats on sale were for children. I continued my search and came across a few sports jackets for women, but I was really looking for a pea coat or something appropriate for work. After tirelessly searching through every rack, I finally found an extra small coat that would have to do. The sale price was exactly fifty dollars, and I was thrilled that my persistence paid off. If I had only stayed in the women's section, I would have never found it, as it was located in the men's section beneath a Ski jacket. The extra-small, camel-colored faux suede coat with a wool lining wasn't the coat I had in mind, but it was better than wearing a sweater or a lightweight blazer in the snow. When I tried it on, the sleeves felt very snug, but with temperatures dipping to twenty degrees, I needed to make it work.

By the time of the next big manager meeting, I managed to save enough money to buy a real suit that actually fit me. I no longer needed homemade alterations or tons of pins. I was also able to carry a small, cute purse since I didn't have to hide any bulges. While it wasn't fancy or tailored, the shades of navy matched, and it looked better than anything I had ever worn.

After fixing my hair weave and applying my fuchsia lipstick, I started to feel pretty good. However, my camel-colored coat didn't quite match my outfit. As always, I arrived at the meeting early. While waiting in my car, I called my cheerleader mom for the reassurance I desperately needed. I told her how confident I felt without the coat, but as soon as I put it on, I felt unprofessional. The sleeves were so snug that I could barely pull the coat over my blazer. Again, Mom reassured me, telling me that everything would be okay.

She suggested I take the coat off and drape it over my arm. I thanked her for her time, exited my car and proceeded to walk to the building with the coat draped over my arm. I only had a few more steps to take before I made it inside without anyone seeing me. No one noticed my fake coat that didn't match my outfit. My makeup was just right, and my jewelry, which I spent under ten bucks on, sparkled like a million bucks.

I was growing... I was flowing... I was movin' and shakin'!!

After a short period of time, TQ and I started dating again. I would either spend the night at his house in Jersey or he would spend the night at my place in PA. We learned that any successful relationship must have God as the foundation. We agreed to keep God first and allow one another to be individuals. When we were younger, I was his girl and he was my man. We were so consumed with each other that we lost ourselves along the way. WE are back on track and stronger than ever.

"What therefore God has joined together, let no man put asunder." Mark 10:9, KJV.

"Whoso findeth a wife findeth a good thing, and obtaineth favour of the LORD." Prov 18:22, KJV.

"Wives, submit yourselves unto your own husband, as unto the Lord." Eph 5:22, KJV.

I worked extremely hard as an office manager. I was understaffed and faced extremely challenging expectations, yet I managed to exceed them while never compromising my integrity. I used to say, "Tie my hands behind my back, bind my legs, and I will still exceed expectations." No matter what was thrown at me, I took it all in my stride because anything was better than the years I spent living in despair.

After a year and a half, I was promoted to a higher-level office manager position. In this role, I would be responsible for managing a much larger team and face greater challenges. I ranked number one in the region and continued to excel in my work. My salary improved significantly, and I no longer had to wear ill-fitting clothes. I was able to pay off my student loans and manage my monthly expenses, with extra money left over. I even enjoyed taking a few nice family vacations each year and dining at upscale restaurants. I received consistent salary increases and continued to advance in my career.

The people who once intimidated me were now inviting me to lunch. I was in a good place. I was happy; I was making it.

After two years in this role, where I led an engaged team, I was presented with an even greater opportunity. I successfully negotiated my new salary and accepted the promotion. This new location was the most challenging I had encountered thus far. The clientele was very different from what I was accustomed to, and I faced greater difficulties in managing my new team. I am grateful for every challenge, setback, and obstacle I encountered. I thank God for every moment when I struggled with self-love, as well as for the times I was lied on and gossiped about. If it weren't for those challenges, I would never have discovered the inspiration to birth,

"I'm Happy Being Me!"

CHAPTER NINE

God did it!

February 10th was one of the worst days of my life, but it also had its silver lining. On this day, my father went to be with the Lord. At 4:30 PM, I received a call from my mom, informing me that Daddy was in the hospital and that I needed to come quickly. I wasn't overly alarmed, as my dad had been in and out of hospice care for over three years before he passed. I assumed he just wasn't doing well and that I should visit him.

We all gathered in his room as family members from all over traveled to meet us at the hospital. I looked at my aunt, and she said, "Baby, your daddy isn't going to make it." I looked at her in terror. I couldn't believe what she said to me. My dad was surrounded by my mother, his daughters, his son, Tarquin, grandchildren, sisters, nieces, and nephews. I watched the machine with the wavy lines and thought that there must be a mistake. We sang songs of praises and told him how much we love him. I was hugging TQ as hard as I could while holding Drew's hands.

The nurses counted down and that night at 9:10 PM my dad's spirit went to be with the Lord.

It was the worst day of my life because my dad was the glue of our family. He kept everyone together and ensured we were at peace. No one had to worry when he was around. However, it was also a good day because my dad can now rest in peace.

The place he has gone to offers freedom from pain, bills, and stress. There are no loud hospital machines or nurses coming in and out of his room. I find peace in knowing that two days before he passed, I visited him in the hospital. I told him that if he was tired and needed to go, it was okay. I assured him that we would all work together to take care of Mom. I also confirmed that he accepted Jesus Christ as his Lord and Savior.

My dad stuck around as long as he did out of concern for my mom. They had great admiration and respect for one another and raised three girls in a happy home. Mom has tough days and I can only imagine her pain, but she's strong. Mom is well-loved and knows that she will see Dad again. When the trumpet blows he will keep a place warm for her. Daddy didn't leave us. He is with us in spirit and his memory will last forever. My father had a wonderful home-going service and his memory will live on!

Throughout my career, my parents have been my greatest cheerleaders and supporters. My dad approached every challenge with a calm demeanor. No matter how difficult I described a situation, he always reassured me that everything would be okay, and it always turned out that way. His go-to response to any challenge was, "No problem!" I held onto every word my dad spoke and continued to persevere, but everything changed drastically when he went to be with the Lord.

When I faced major challenges at work, I no longer had him to call for support. However, I am grateful for the lessons he had instilled in me; they helped me persevere most of the time. I also had my own methods for staying motivated. Each morning, I listened to inspirational music and messages for at least fifteen minutes before getting out of bed. Once I was up, I continued the positive mindset by listening to gospel music and reciting affirmations while getting dressed. During my drive to work, I took time to pray. Some days were so taxing that I found myself listening to positive affirmations while using the bathroom at work. During the most challenging moments, I placed several Post-it notes on the walls of my home office to combat the negative emotions I was experiencing.

On each wall were messages on Post-it notes that read inspirations such as, "Never stop being YOU" "I am more than a conqueror." "I'm blessed… it's a matter of time before things change, this is temporary." "I am the talent; I have what it takes." "I made it." "I'm good enough." Sometimes, I even wrote positive affirmations with lipstick on all my mirrors. Sometimes, I would leave messages on my son's bathroom mirror, even though I never used that bathroom myself. I wanted to spare him the feelings of dread and hopelessness that I had once experienced, so I thought of it as a way to help prevent him from facing the harsh realities of life.

I thank God for all the affirmations I read over the years. Eventually, they became a part of me, and I was strong enough to remove them from my walls and mirrors.

If I experienced extreme anxiety, I practiced 'Mirror Talk,' which involves looking deep into my eyes in the mirror and reminding myself of how far I've come and how strong I am. I would say out of my mouth, "Wendy, you got this, you have to keep going," sometimes while even wiping the tears from my eyes. My favorite phrase of encouragement was and continues to be, "The best is yet to come."

Faith that things would always get better gave me the courage to keep going, even when tears were running down my cheeks during my most uncertain moments. I knew that I could never allow myself to give up, as I had come too far to turn back.

My positive mindset usually kept me going, but on this particular day, I just couldn't shake the feeling of defeat.

No matter what I tried—who I spoke to or what I listened to—the heaviness I felt wouldn't lift. On this very day, I particularly crossed every T and dotted every I. I did much more than what was expected of me, yet I still fell short of the goal that was set. In that moment, I failed to recognize my own greatness and overlooked the progress I had made. Feelings of being undervalued and unworthy began to surface once again.

While sitting at my dining room table all alone after working over ten hours and not having more than fifteen minutes for lunch, I didn't have any pep in my pep talk. I cried out to God; I often speak to Him… I said, "God, I know You created me for more than this. I don't believe anyone has the right to beat me down if I have given my all. I'm tired and feel defeated. Please give me strength."

"God, I need you to reveal my talent." For the next few moments, I openly and freely shared my pain with God. I shared how people talked behind my back and started rumors about me, that people constantly criticized my enthusiasm… I shared that half the people who smiled and had great conversations with me were the same people who spoke negatively when not in my presence. I shared how I was called fake because they don't know my story or understand my joy. I expressed how empty I felt after losing my father and my concerns for my mom. After pouring my heart out to God, I immediately picked up my pen and began to write. I thought about children and adults who are also feeling overwhelmed, mistreated, hopeless, or unappreciated. I reflected on the pain I experienced during my teenage years and the struggles that many children are currently facing. A wave of emotions washed over me as I sat alone at my table. If our children grow up feeling broken and do not find healing and support, they may become broken adults who, in turn, raise broken children, continuing the cycle. I want to break that cycle. The first words on my paper were, "I like to wear dresses; I am pretty as can be, God has made me special, and I am Happy Being Me."

I once worked in an environment that claimed to accept and celebrate differences, yet I was constantly criticized for being just that. My pen began moving more quickly. The next line read, "I like my furry friend; we run, we jump and we play. We have a fun-filled happy dance, we dance and dance all day."

My desire is for people to love and embrace their uniqueness because the aspects that distinguish us also make us special. Everyone has the right to be happy while embracing their full peculiarity. Society places immense pressure to fit into their little boxes. I choose to break free because, "We don't need to fit in someone else's box when we can create our own." Are ya with me?

Having personally experienced the pain of exclusion and relentless criticism from those who never took the time to understand me, I am determined to use my experiences and passion to prevent others from feeling the same way. By the time I reached the fifth sentence, I had made the decision to write a book. I praised and thanked God for His assistance as my pen flowed freely across the paper. By the end of that night, my book was complete. I was going to be an author! I wasn't sure how or when it would happen, but I knew that the feeling I experienced that day was something I wanted to embrace forever. I allowed my pain to fuel my purpose, and so can you!

After the words of my book were completed, I began to envision the cover filled with diverse children. I created a few sketches, and picked out some color schemes while reflecting on the night, I decided to be an author. When I grew tired of trying to prove my identity and worth, I realized that I had many more talents than I was currently using. I loved my company and my job, but I knew I was more than just an office manager. I wanted to pursue my dream of becoming a published author. Once I had my ideas for the book format written down, I began searching online for qualified illustrators. However, each time I thought I had found the right person, I ended up disappointed. After reviewing their credentials and samples, I noticed that none of them met my expectations. I provided detailed instructions to each potential artist, but they were unable to create the images I envisioned.

I eventually connected with an artist who seemed to be the perfect fit for my project. I shared my vision and provided detailed instructions for the opening page, which was meant to feature a Hispanic girl twirling her dress on the playground. After a few days, I received an image of a Caucasian girl wearing pants and surrounded by trees. I expressed my dissatisfaction with the image and requested that the artist deliver what I had originally paid for. The following day, she sent me another image of a Caucasian princess wearing a pink, flowy gown and a crown. Although the character was different, the background still featured trees, but she added a swing. I was disappointed once again and asked for a full refund. After several days of back-and-forth communication, she eventually agreed to refund my money.

I was back to the search. After several weeks of wasting time and money, I finally found someone! I was very pleased with Fred's reviews, experience, samples and rates. The image of the Hispanic girl twirling her dress he provided was more beautiful than I could have ever imagined. I provided a portion of the book for him to draw at a time, and each time, he exceeded my expectations. He was professional, followed directions, and delivered the work in a timely manner. He seemed to understand my vision and helped bring it to life. After a series of disappointing searches, I finally found someone I could count on. However, after completing two pages, Fred suddenly fell ill and could no longer continue the project. After months of time and money invested, the illustrator who had the ability to complete the tasks was no longer available to assist. A sense of rejection washed over me once again, and I began to overanalyze every conversation we had. I wondered if perhaps I had done something to upset him. Maybe I was too assertive? Maybe I was asking for too much? How did he suddenly come down with an illness? I realized that I was professional, provided clear, concise instructions, and paid on time. I knew I didn't do anything wrong, so I accepted that it was back to the drawing board. I could no longer use the images that I paid for and waited several weeks to receive because I wanted all the images to be uniformed. His style of art was difficult to duplicate.

The following week, I reached out to a couple of schools and local artists. Most of them were unreliable. When I asked for samples, they committed to providing them on specific dates and times and never sent them. Each time I followed up, they responded with nothing but excuses. I already wasted money and time and was ready to work with someone I could count on. The few artists who did in fact provide samples in a timely manner, were unable to provide what I needed.

Finding an illustrator became a second job. Day and night, night and day, I searched, connected, became excited, then was let down time and time again. After tirelessly searching for an artist, I decided to ask God to send me a Christian illustrator who could not only understand my vision but also expand upon it. I stopped stressing and obsessing over the search and let go of late-night searches.

Once I embraced and trusted the process, I stumbled across my current illustrator, Ms. Jas. I gave her the same details for my opening page: a Hispanic girl twirling her dress in a park. To my delight, Jas quickly sent me the image I had requested. She executed it perfectly, and her illustrations turned out to be even better than those of Fred, my previous illustrator. I initially believed that nothing could exceed Fred's work, but not only did Ms. Jas include every detail I requested, she also added some wonderful personal touches that I absolutely love! Each time I described my vision she executed and added her special touch. I felt as if she was in my mind and was able to see everything that I saw. I would send her samples of my scribbles along with a few descriptions, and she would make them a trillion times better. She is my "Godsent." I described the special day when my dad removed the training wheels from my bike, which can be found on pages eighteen and nineteen of my published children's self- esteem book, I'm Happy Being Me. She knew exactly what I needed…. all the way down to the details of the clothes, my bike, and my hair. She even nailed the image of my father after I provided sample pictures of him. Every interaction with her involved mutual encouragement and support for each other's success. Her work has been published worldwide. I am truly grateful for the opportunity to collaborate with her.

I had my manuscript, illustrations, and an eye-catching book cover, but I was still far from the finish line. I shared the process of creating my book with a close friend I've known for over twenty-five years, Indonesia. Her response was, "Go for it!" She's the kind of woman who loves deeply and wholeheartedly. If she considers you a friend, you are truly blessed to have her in your life. She was one of my biggest supporters at the beginning of my book journey and continued to be throughout the process. No matter what time of night I called, she was always willing to listen to my ideas and offer words of encouragement, love, and genuine support.

I researched many publishing companies during this time. A few expressed interest in working with me after reviewing my manuscript, but each time I read the fine print to the best of my ability, it seemed that they wanted to own part of my book in some sort of way or would charge a very high rate for printing. A few companies suggested that my book would be more successful if I removed the word "God," but I couldn't do that. God has been with me in my darkest hour. He assisted me every step of the way. How dare I remove His name. Still, no success with finding a publishing company.

I typically woke up around 5:30 AM and would lie in bed, mentally preparing myself for a challenging day at work. I usually arrived home around 7:30 PM, spent a few moments with my family, and then continued my research until about 1:00 AM. Thank goodness for coffee around that time of my life… It kept me going when I ran out of steam. Despite the numerous meetings and phone conversations I had, I felt uncomfortable partnering with any company I interacted with, particularly if it meant authorizing them to make changes. I knew their ultimate goal would be to remove the word "God" from my book. Unsure of how to proceed, I decided to have another conversation with God. My exact words were, "God, I have no idea what I am doing, but you gave me this passion and vision, so I need you to send the right people."

Shortly after my conversation with God, I was introduced to Mrs. Kimberly McGill. I was told that she is extremely knowledgeable in the business field and could potentially be a great resource to utilize. My first conversation with Mrs. McGill lasted over an hour. What I was told about her was right; she was in fact very direct, but also a great listener and a wonderful encourager. I love the fact that Mrs. McGill is God-fearing, well-informed and straight to the point. Our very first call felt more like a job interview. Pastor Kim gave me a list of things I should work on to enhance my business and I held on to her every word. When I hung up with her, I felt mentally exhausted but so very excited that she shared her precious time and valuable information. Each time I needed assistance, she made herself available. While expressing sincere gratitude towards her for her expertise, she replied by saying, "You're going to do all of the work; I'll just provide information."

No matter what I did to thank her, she only responded by saying, "God gets all of the glory." I was impressed by her level of humility. When I asked her why she was so open to helping me, she said that "I was her assignment" and that she had a great level of respect for the person who referred me to her. Each time we spoke on the phone, my confidence increased. No matter what astronomical goal I set regarding my book and organization, she always responded with, "Okay… let's do it!" Because she was so committed to fulfilling her assignment and had so much faith in my book, my faith in my book also increased.

Before I knew it, I had organized a book review for my family, asking them to provide their honest feedback.

I explained that their task was to identify any errors and give constructive criticism before my book was released to the world. After completing their feedback forms, everything was ready for the press.

I've learned about self-publishing through firsthand experience. I can't express how much research I conducted, how many YouTube videos I watched, and how many hours I spent soaking up wisdom from published authors. I am grateful for the many individuals who offered their prayers, encouragement, and support along the way.

I would like to give a special thank you to Mrs. Adrienne Taylor, who showed immense interest in the "Happy Being Me" movement. Not only did she purchase copies of my work and support my music video and radio appearances, but she also prayed for me during times when I felt insecure. Her encouragement filled me with power, confidence, and inspiration! She consistently reminded me that with God, all things are possible and cheered for my success, which kept me going during moments of uncertainty. I am truly thankful for my dear Adrienne (Queen); she is truly a gem!

While working on the book publishing process, I started my own business. After considering several names, I decided on "Someone Cares About Me LLC." I chose this name because knowing that someone truly cares about me gave me the courage to keep pushing forward. I wanted to provide that same encouragement to others. During my darkest moments, I reflected on the love and support from my parents, husband, and son. Their care helped me feel less isolated, as I realized there were people cheering for me. If the community knows that someone cares about them, they may be more willing to fight for their survival, just as I did. Praise be to God,

I also established a registered non-profit organization, 501(c)(3) called Happy Being Me Inc. because it's important to love every part of yourself and to find happiness in doing so. We need to recognize that the traits that make us peculiar are also the traits that make us special.

My first cousin, Antonio, whom we affectionately call Boss, was born an "angel." He is featured in my book, 'I'm Happy Being Me' on page seventeen. Whenever I visited him, Boss always made me feel special and appreciated. As soon as I walked in the door, he would call out my name, Nee Nee, with enthusiasm and give me a big hug and kiss. My aunt and uncle were unaware that sometimes, when I felt down, I would stop by their house just to receive a hug from Boss. His heart is pure and authentic, and being around that type of positive energy can uplift you when you're feeling low. Knowing that Boss and my family love me unconditionally has greatly influenced the title of my business, 'Someone Cares About Me.' Their care, support, and love gave me a reason to fight, a reason to live, and a reason to thrive. The name of my organization holds profound meaning for me; the compassion of others truly has the power to move mountains.

Once I was satisfied with my business name, I dedicated the same amount of time and effort to creating my logo. I wanted my logo to symbolize love and unity. Once again, I prayed for guidance. After several weeks of doodling, I created an image that I was pleased with. I then sent this image to an artist for refinement. After finalizing the design, I submitted the finished image to the copyright office and moved on to the next task.

My goal for my organization is to promote healing and provide all the resources I needed as a child. While my parents loved me dearly, I lacked connections to mentors or support groups outside my home. Because of this, I took the initiative to create those opportunities for those in need.

'Someone Cares About Me LLC' is here to help you live life to the fullest! Our goal is to provide you with all the necessary tools to overcome any obstacles that come your way and to help you be your best self. We believe that everyone should be free to express their true selves without any barriers holding them back. So, let us offer you a helping hand and provide the resources you need to support you on your journey toward fulfillment and authenticity!

We offer workshops on anti-bullying coaching and intervention strategies tailored for teachers and administrators. These workshops equip staff to recognize signs of harassment and respond effectively to reports of bullying, thereby fostering trust and rapport with students. When students feel connected and trusted by faculty, they are more likely to share information and report instances of bullying. Effective communication is key!

In addition to our self-esteem and anti-bullying programs, we also provide an introductory job readiness workshop. This workshop covers essential topics including interviewing skills and techniques, telephone etiquette, business etiquette, empowerment, networking to create opportunities, and maintaining professionalism.
About Happy Being Me…

Our Mission:

Happy Being Me, Inc. focuses on building confidence and success in both children and adults through personalized coaching and group strategy sessions. Our goal is to foster leadership qualities and nurture each individual's unique strengths in a safe, non-judgmental environment where positivity and resilience can thrive.
To learn more visit:
www.someonecaresaboutme.com

CHAPTER TEN

Happy Being Me

Within six months of starting my journey, I found myself sitting at my dining room table, holding a physical copy of my book in my hands. I couldn't believe it! I prayed over every single book, asking God to bless each person who would read it. I am grateful to share my father's legacy with everyone who purchases a copy. This feels like a way to keep his memory alive. It's incredible how much strength I receive from those who believe in me. On the back cover of the book, my dad is looking down from heaven at his four flowers: my mom, Ros, Lisa, and me. I quickly sold out of my first batch of books solely through word of mouth; I had no storefront or online presence. It was just me, my passion, a few good friends, and the grace of God. The numerous reviews I received about how my book changed children's lives affirmed my purpose. I finally began living the life I had only dreamed of.

A year after my book was released, I wrote and directed my first professional music video titled "I'm Happy Being Me." The video was filmed at the school where I had experienced bullying as a child. On the morning of the video shoot, everything that could possibly go wrong did. While I was driving to Jersey, I not only had one flat tire but two. I found myself sitting on the side of the road, starting to panic because, as the director, I needed to arrive before the cast to set up. While I was there, a police officer pulled up. I worried he would give me a hard time since I was parked illegally and blocking traffic. I explained to him the importance of my music video.

"Oh, I'm really sorry to hear that," he said, his voice filled with genuine sympathy. "I need to get there before anyone else!" I told the officer, my voice laced with panic. He smiled at me with kindness. "Why don't you leave your car by the side of the road?" he suggested, meeting my gaze.

I stared back at him, and my heart felt heavier. The thought of leaving my car by the side of the road with no one to look after it made me feel uneasy. The man, as if he could read my mind and the fear I was feeling, grinned at me. "Come on, ma'am. Don't worry about your car. While you're away, I'll keep an eye on it for you."

I was astonished. He was a stranger yet was willing to help me. "Really?" I asked him. "Of course! I can see that you are a woman with a golden heart." He flashed me a smile, and I couldn't help but smile back. I thanked the kind officer and got out of the car, my eyes filled with appreciation for his kindness.

I called one of my cast members, who was a few minutes behind TQ and me. When he arrived a few minutes later, we continued with our plans for the day. I received a great deal of support from TQ, Quan, Natosha, Pastor Kim, Drew, India, Anissa, Adrienne, Brian, my mom, family, and friends. I walked through the same halls, looked at the same lockers, and even sat in the same classroom where I was bullied over twenty-five years ago. I entered my school, but this time I had a voice—a voice of strength of my own and a voice of strength for others who have yet to find theirs.

We only had eight hours to shoot the video, and despite several hiccups along the way, we managed to accomplish our goal. Once the shoot was complete, I contacted my insurance company to request a tow for my car to my mechanic. The following day, I called the mechanic to ask them to fix my tires, only to be informed that my car had never been towed there. After going back and forth with the insurance company for over two hours, they admitted that they had lost my car. It wasn't until seventy-two hours later that I realized my car had never been towed at all and was still sitting on the side of the road across the bridge in New Jersey.

I managed to resolve the issue and kept movin' & shakin'!

Our music video is now available on YouTube!

Check out "Wendy Inspire" and be sure to subscribe.

Title: World Premiere! Happy Being Me Music Video

Here's what I've been through to get to this point:

- Born peculiar
- Struggled with low self-esteem
- Severely bullied
- Physically, mentally, and emotionally beaten
- Lied on
- Cheated on
- Used and abused
- Never fit in

Use your pain to fuel your passion. God has no respect of person. I promise if He did it for me He will surely do the same for you!

I encourage you to take some time to reflect on your life, especially your darkest moments. Remember the time when she left you feeling alone and confused, the time when you were homeless, and the time when you sold drugs, sold your body, spent time in jail, lost your best friend or was abused. Think back to the time you were betrayed... the time when you wanted to give up... Yet "YOU" are still standing! That goes to show that you have purpose! There is a reason you made it when others in your situation didn't.

Don't let another day go by without doing something that makes you happy, because you matter. You deserve happiness! Allow your challenges to make you stronger. Step away from the pain and seek the lessons within it. After all, life is a test. When you pass your current round, you have the opportunity to move on to the next one, which may be even more challenging. Be sure to take a moment to pause and reflect on the lessons. If you fail to pass your current test, you'll continue facing the same lesson until you learn what you need to proceed to the next stage, and the cycle will repeat.

When I was a little girl, I had dolls in shades of brown and apricot. Although I was taught that everyone is beautiful and special, I never found dolls with hair like mine. As a teenager, I began adding length to my hair by using braid extensions or adding a few extra tracks to my ponytail for fullness. My obsession with hair weaves didn't really begin until my late twenties, and it continued into my late thirties. I let the messages I received from the world around me shape my perception of beauty. My idea of beauty was heavily influenced by the glamour magazines I saw while waiting in checkout lines, which featured girls who looked nothing like me. Additionally, my social media feeds were flooded with images of women with long, flowing hair. The primary source of my "pretty girl obsession" was rooted in my childhood experiences. The dark-skinned girls who disliked me constantly called me ugly, and I believed them. However, once I turned sixteen, many people began to tell me that I was beautiful and looked like a movie star. I even had a few friends who nicknamed me "Hollywood." Despite their compliments, I didn't believe

I was gorgeous, but I worked hard to meet their expectations. I wanted to be accepted so badly that I spent several hours each morning trying to look like Barbie as much as possible. I spared no expense when it came to my hair weave, spending close to eight hundred dollars on my initial installation. This included two bundles of eighteen-inch virgin hair, which lasted roughly two years, along with the cost of installation. Every strand of my hair had to be perfectly styled, and I absolutely needed to have a heavy swoop bang. If the weight of my bang wasn't sufficient, my stylist had to continue adding more hair until there was absolutely no space left.

Once my weave was installed, I examined every follicle to ensure that every strand was placed in the proper direction. Not only did my hair cost a pretty penny, but my pursuit of perfection came at a higher price. It cost me my happiness and freedom, for sure. I didn't realize how deeply bound I was until I made it to the other side (All praises be to The Most High!).

During family gatherings, my cousin-brother Drew would roughhouse with his boys and our relatives. I watched everyone running around, happy and free, laughing and smiling. However, I was too afraid to join in because I didn't want to get sweaty, and I certainly didn't want to mess up my perfectly styled hair. I hated being outdoors on humid days since it ruined my hair and makeup. Even when I worked out during the winter months, I would turn on the air conditioning and a fan at the same time because I refused to sweat my hair out.

While my family enjoyed swimming in Drew's pool, I sat far enough away to avoid getting splashed. Instead of joining in, I observed my family while sipping a glass of wine, too afraid to risk ruining the look I had spent hours perfecting.

My morning routine consisted of:

1. Waking up and thanking The Most High for another day
2. Brushing my teeth for at least sixty seconds (twice)
3. Gargle with salt water
4. Gargle with mouthwash
5. Shower for about fifteen minutes, any longer would mess up my hair even if I wore a shower cap. While in the shower—exfoliate face, hands and feet
6. Allow my face to air dry or use a paper towel to attempt to mitigate breakouts
7. Apply a thin layer of foundation

After applying the first layer of foundation, I sat in front of the fan for about two minutes to help it set. Once it was dry, I repeated this process up to two more times. For special occasions, I use my makeup airbrush to achieve an even, flawless glow. About ten minutes before I needed to leave, I would remove my silk scarf and gently run my fingers through my weave. Then, I would take my paddle brush to ensure that the top section around my bangs was perfectly styled. Once I finished with my weave, I applied edge control to my hairline, and then I was ready to go.

Before I left my driveway, I checked my purse to ensure I didn't forget my small makeup bag, which contained all my makeup essentials, especially my twenty-four-hour color stay foundation. I really didn't need it, but just liked knowing it was there.

After taking my lunch break, I brushed my teeth using the toothpaste and toothbrush I kept in my desk drawer at work. Once I finished brushing, I applied either glassy gloss, clear lip gloss, or my favorite tube of fuchsia lipstick. The only times I went without lipstick were when I was eating or sleeping. Being pretty seemed to work for me; it made me feel in control. All the girls who bullied me as a child wanted to be my friend as an adult. When I was out and about, people tended to be much nicer to me when I looked pretty.

Many people have told me that I possess a great personality, a pretty face, and a nice figure. As a result, I made it a point to wear form-fitting clothes to feel accepted. However, I never opted for daisy dukes or tops that exposed cleavage. My standard attire typically consisted of a simple, form-fitting dress paired with six-inch heels and a designer bag. For many years, I invested a significant amount of effort into my appearance because I felt it was all I had to offer.

For over fifteen years, I was in bondage without even realizing it. My self-esteem was dependent on my outward appearance. Each day, my goal was to look as much like a Black Barbie as possible. There was a time in my twenties when I did Tae Bo twice a day, meticulously measured every portion of my food, and occasionally took laxatives to maintain the small amount of weight I had. I was born petite and have always been on the thinner side. As a teenager, I weighed between one hundred and one hundred fifteen pounds. As an adult, I averaged around one hundred thirty pounds. Although I was never considered overweight, I believed that weighing one hundred pounds or less was the standard of beauty, at least according to many fashion magazines back then.

When I reached one hundred and three pounds, I would take a laxative because I believed that thin equaled beauty. TQ did not know I was taking an occasional laxative, but he did notice I was dropping weight fast. After I started experiencing nausea and extreme headaches, I stopped. My laxative abuse lasted a few months.

Every two weeks, I was in the nail salon getting my gel mani-pedi. I never allowed my fingernails or toenails to breathe without polish. Even during winter, when most women allowed their toenails to have a break, I faithfully kept paint on top of mine.

I used to wake up a few hours before my husband to shower, apply makeup, brush my teeth, and do my hair. After that, I would lie back in bed and "pretend" that I looked flawless twenty-four hours a day. I must say, I applaud my effort and dedication, but it really doesn't take all that!

Wearing my natural hair blown out and straightened by the Dominicans literally made my hair so straight that if you saw me from the back, you would have thought I was Caucasian. I loved it because I thought that my hair would only be beautiful if it were straightened. I allowed the stylists to burn my hair to the point where my entire car smelled like burnt hair while driving home from the salon. The heat they used on my hair was too high for frequent visits to their shop, but I did it because I believed I wouldn't be beautiful without straight hair. Constantly flat-ironing my hair at the Dominicans left it fragile. The health of my hair was severely damaged primarily due to frequent visits. My hair was flowy but brittle and felt like paper. Each morning, when I combed it, I saw at least fifteen long, thick strands fall into my sink.

My addiction to hair weaves was so extreme that I would have them removed, washed, and reinstalled all on the same day. I never allowed my scalp to rest or breathe because I believed I was only pretty if my hair looked like the glamorous styles I saw on TV. After many years of wearing hair weaves, my hairline became very thin. At first, I didn't care; I thought I could just add a larger bang to camouflage it. However, after watching several YouTube videos of women who went permanently bald due to hair weaves, I realized I needed to change my habits. I started to give my hair a break between installations. My "weave abuse" had caused my hair to lose its luster and shine.

After filming my music video, I reflected on the image I wanted to portray to the little girls watching. Did I want to continue presenting a "false" sense of beauty, or did I want to show them that I am genuinely happy being me? Did I want to add extra pressure on women to be perfect, or did I want to demonstrate that there is freedom in embracing who we are meant to be? Shortly after the shoot, I looked in the mirror and said out loud, "Wendy, this is not you anymore."

I no longer saw myself as beautiful with someone else's hair attached to my head. In that moment, through my own eyes, I appeared to be lost. I called my stylist, who is not associated with the Dominican Hair Salon, and told her I wanted to loc my hair. She was my stylist for over six years and completely understood my "highly emotional perfect weave personality" and the hairstyles that made me happiest. She spent countless hours working with that swoop bang of mine and took my calls after hours when I was having a hissy fit about my hair.

"You sure you want to do this?" she asked. I replied, "Yes." Although she was very surprised by my request for such a drastic transformation from Barbie to locs, she said,

"Okay, let's schedule your appointment."

Since I began my locs in July 2018, my life has improved immensely. The term "loc" is derived from "dreadlock," but I choose not to refer to my hair as "dreadlocks" or " dreads" because those names are rooted in racial persecution and discrimination. Europeans used the term "dreadlock" because they viewed the loc'd hair of people of color as a "dreadful sight." However, there is absolutely nothing dreadful about the hair that God created for me. I have come to realize that I am beautiful just as He made me. In the past, I felt like I was insulting God by manipulating my hair to conform to others' standards. If He wanted my hair to be long and straight, He would have created it that way. I came to realize that frequently altering my hair's natural state suggested that what He had blessed me with wasn't good enough. This understanding made me feel that my efforts to change my hair were a sign of ingratitude. So, I decided to embrace my hair in its natural form and experience complete FREEdom.

For the first time since my childhood, my husband and family can touch my hair without me freaking out. I no longer worry about the weather or the level of humidity. I no longer rush out of the shower, out of fear of messing up my hair. As I became closer to The Most High, I realized that He is the only one who defines beauty. We are all fearfully and wonderfully made just as we are. We don't need to buy someone's hair, inject foreign substances, or associate with a particular crowd to be valuable. I've come to realize that true beauty lies in authenticity. It's about embracing the natural texture of my hair and wearing modest clothing, all while radiating joy, peace, and freedom. I was overly concerned about being accepted by everyone, but as I grow, I realize that I was not created to fit with everyone, nor should I want to.

The transition was initially challenging because I was still a little concerned about how others would perceive me. However, this time I chose not to let those worries hold me back from breaking free from my constraints. When I finally saw my hair in its completely natural state for the first time since childhood, I cried! After having my locs installed, I looked in the mirror and truly saw myself. I noticed my smile, my beautiful light brown eyes, my teeth, and many other details about my face that I had neglected to appreciate while I was focused on trying to make my hair look like everyone else's.

The day I loc'd my hair, another chain was broken. I've never felt freer or more empowered. With locs, there is no fuss and no major maintenance, and my hair is becoming thicker and healthier. The burnt smell from my hair being fried by the Dominicans went away after two months of having my locs and my pillows and scarves no longer smell like a fire pit. I threw out most of my hair products because I no longer need them. Wooo Hooo! Getting ready for work in the morning is now a breeze.

In the morning, I simply remove my silk scarf, spray the ends of my hair with water, shake my hair a bit and off I go. This is yet another step of my growth!

I don't wanna' be perfect, I wanna' be me!

The only way to truly be free is to share your truth. People may judge you no matter how many things you get right. So, you might as well be true to yourself and do what makes you happy. You may not see the struggles I've faced just by looking at me, but I have been through a lot. So, be kind, avoid rushing to judgment, and live the best life you possibly can!

HalleluYah! Praise God! I'm FREE! I made it!

Now you know my story

Now you know more of me

Now you know why I stand before you

"HAPPY BEING ME"

01-17-19   5:53 AM

Dear friend,
Who would have thought life would be
so challenging as an adult... If we
would have only known I'm sure most
of us would not have been in such a
hurry to grow up. Sometimes we look
around and say... "this is it?"
My answer to your question is, NO...
This is not it. It is not the end. There
is so much more to do. Each and every
one of us is born with a gift or talent,
but less than half us of us ever truly
tap into it. I want you to grab the
bull by the horns and live! No more
just existing... It's your time to thrive!
It's your time to soar! You are far greater
than you give yourself credit for... You
are WORTHY and you matter. Don't
allow another day to go by watching
others fulfill their dreams when you have
the ability to win along with them!
Keep going my friend!

The best is yet to come!

See ya at the top!

♡
Wendy

**All materials are crafted by a human,
inspired and guided by the Wisdom
of the Holy Spirit, who offered insight
and clarity throughout the process.**